Witch Tips

The Essential Guide to Contemporary Witchcraft

A. Rayne

With Illustrations by Eugenia Rocha Méndez

Copyright © 2018 by Austyn Castelli

All rights reserved. No part of this publication may be reproduced, distributed, or transmitted in any form or by any means, including photocopying, recording, or other electronic or mechanical methods, without the prior written permission of the publisher, except in the case of brief quotations embodied in critical reviews and certain other noncommercial uses permitted by copyright law.

ISBN-13: 978-1721695393
ISBN-10: 1721695397

Any references to historical events, real people, or real places are purely coincidental.

Front cover image by May Phan
Illustrations by Eugenia Rocha Mendez

Printed by CreateSpace LLC

First Printing Edition 2018

The guide is dedicated to the abnormal, the curious, and the strange. When you cannot find a place in the world, make your own.

Introduction..1

Basics 12

    Energy...13

    Element..16

    Crystals..19

    Herbs, Flowers, and Plants............................29

    Fruit, Vegetables, and Food Magick................49

    Color Correspondences...................................52

    Animal Correspondences................................54

    Spellcasting..61

    Symbols...65

    Tools..66

    Spell Types..69

    Sachets, Potions, and Jar Spells....................73

    Moon Phases, Times, and Days of the Week....75

    Divination...79

    Spirit Work..88

    Technology-Based Witchcraft 95

The World of Witchcraft 97

    Classifications of Witches...............................98

    Religion and Witchcraft 104

    Altars..106

    Sabbats...107

Familiars..........113
Covens..........114

Spells..........118
Tips..........136
Frequently Asked Questions..........145
Glossary of Terms..........152

Introduction

Witchcraft has a long and sordid history. The practice has gone through times of popularity and persecution. Luckily, modern times have begun to trend toward an overall acceptance of modern Witchcraft practices. As more progressive generations arise so do we see a rise in those who explore religions and spiritual practices outside of the one(s) that they were brought up in.

What many people do not realize about Witchcraft is that it is not a religion, but rather a spiritual practice that can be observed alongside many different religions. Many modern-day Witches choose to practice Witchcraft in combination with traditional religions such as Christianity, Judaism, and Buddhism.

As in other popular spiritual practices, there are many branches and "brands" of Witchcraft . Wicca and Paganism have traditionally been synonymous with Witchcraft . However, both are their own complete religions that each incorporate certain aspects of Witchcraft in their belief systems. This guide will focus on non-theistic Witchcraft , which can be practiced on its own or with other religious tenets.

The main difference between non-theistic Witchcraft and the aforementioned religion-based practices is the absence of one or more deities. In this way, non-theistic Witchcraft is heavily nature based with many rituals and Sabbats based upon the changing of seasons and properties of the earth and its place in the galaxy.

A Word About Inclusion

Any person can practice Witchcraft regardless of race, religion, gender identity, sexual or romantic orientation, or disability. It can be practiced alone or socially and can be adapted to anyone's personal needs. This being the case, many Witchcraft practitioners find solace and community through their craft that they have been unable to find elsewhere. Though in any group there will be people who attempt to exclude others, the practice of Witchcraft is malleable and accessible to all who wish to learn it.

It would be a disservice to all to ignore the fact that over the course of the existence of modern Witchcraft there have been some who chose to base their practice on outdated misogynistic and racist beliefs. A modern Witch has a duty to recognize these insidious particles within literature and practice.

On a similar note, the presence of cultural appropriation in the Witchcraft community is a topic of great debate. The use of closed practices by Witches of outside cultures as well as the perpetuation of hurtful terms and notions serve only to taint the Witchcraft community as a whole.

Health and Witchcraft

Mental health is a topic of great importance, not just in Witchcraft, but in everyday life as well. In the past, symptoms of various mental conditions were inappropriately attributed to the demonic possession or clairvoyance. It is important to clarify that mental health disorders such as schizophrenia may cause sufferers to have auditory or visual hallucinations as well as physically manifesting symptoms.

As you will learn throughout this book, auditory, sensory, and visual forms of divination are skills that a practitioner chooses to engage in. People who experience hearing voices or seeing strange images involuntarily should seek professional help. Furthermore, the act of exorcism is not to be attempted. In fact, there have been countless instances in which people accused of being possessed have been seriously injured and even killed during unneeded exorcisms.

On a similar note, none of the advice given in the book should be used as a substitution for medical attention or treatment. Herbs and other remedies referenced should always be researched before use and individuals should be aware of their own allergies, sensitivities, and that of their pets or roommates.

The Witchcraft Revival

Witchcraft can be a powerful tool in elevating one's confidence, establishing a feeling of empowerment, and coping with anxiety. This is one of many reasons why the practice of Witchcraft has seen a resurgence in recent years, despite the widespread belief that Witchcraft is "make believe".

The word "Witchcraft ," for most, conjures mental images of pointed hats, broomsticks, and bubbling cauldrons filled with green goo. Witches are thought to be part of the past, and anyone who claims they are one must be delusional, right?

The little-known fact of the matter is this; Witchcraft is a rich spiritual practice that is still very much embraced, in one form or another, by Americans. Now, there are a few basics that one must know about modern Witchcraft :

Witchcraft is not a religion. It can be practiced in tandem with different religions, such as Christianity, Judaism, Hinduism, etc. Wicca is a particular branch of Witchcraft with its own religious tenets. Wicca is a form of Witchcraft, but not all Witchcraft is Wicca.

It's all about energies and nature. The "magic" part of Witchcraft has less to do with shooting electricity from your fingertips than it does with being attuned to the energies of others, nature, objects, and yourself. One of the main beliefs in Witchcraft is that everything contains energy. For example, certain plants and crystals contain calming energies. These objects can be used to help calm someone if they find themselves in an especially anxious mood. The use and manipulation of energies is a central part of Witchcraft.

It is neither good nor bad, it just is. The stereotype that Witchcraft is an "evil" or "satanic" practice is almost completely false. I say almost because each person's Craft is different than the next, meaning if one so chose they could limit their practice to negative or destructive Magick. The vast majority of Witchcraft is positive and used for self-improvement.

So, why has such a practice seen a resurgence within the last decade, especially in

America? In a society so heavily ruled by technology, Witchcraft can seem lackluster and old-fashioned in comparison. Are people drawn to it because it provides an escape from modern culture? Are they drawn to the dark and mysterious aesthetic of it? Do they use it as a way to rebel? The answers vary from person to person. As a longtime Witchcraft practitioner and blogger, here is what I've found from those in the Witchcraft community.

"I was inexplicably drawn to it."

I hear this from many Witches. Sometimes people have an innate fascination with the mysterious or macabre, and Witches are usually one of the first such figures that American children are exposed to. Some become fascinated, not only by the mythology of Witches but by the historical components, like the infamous Salem Witch Trials which took place in the late 1600s in Salem, Massachusetts. Because of the integration of Witches into American culture, it's no wonder that some grow up with an interest in Witchcraft .

"I wanted to be a part of a community."

The Witchcraft community is a vast one, especially online, and is surprisingly harmonious. Within any spiritual practice, there will be various opinions, beliefs, and preferences. This has the potential to cause rifts and divide a community, but the majority of the Witchcraft community understands that Witchcraft is a general and malleable practice that can be shaped to fit every Witch's comfort level and needs. Because of this, there exists a general acceptance within the Witchcraft community.

"It makes me feel powerful and in control."

This is the reason why I got involved in Witchcraft . After living with anxiety and depression for many years and feeling pretty helpless and out of control, learning about and practicing Witchcraft helped me feel safe, powerful, and stable. It also allowed me to become connected to nature and the energies of the world. Because Witchcraft helps one to have a way to control their own energies as well as the energies around them it creates a sense of power and fearlessness that many lack. This is especially important for those with mental illness, those who have survived abuse, those who are disabled, and people of color.

There are hundreds of other reasons that people choose to practice Witchcraft , but what does that have to do with modern America? For starters, many young people in America feel discarded and powerless. We live in a time where around 70% of college students graduate with tuition loan debt and only about 27% of college graduates obtain a job in their field after graduation. Earning money and becoming financially stable has become increasingly more difficult for young people in America.

The battle for social justice has become increasingly heated in recent years and has put people of color and LGBT+ people in dangerous positions within our society. Because of the lack of safety for these groups in public, the online community has become a battleground for the spread of information. It's obvious why Witchcraft would speak to oppressed groups like these. It provides a sense of control in an unstable and uncontrollable society.

Witchcraft is also unabashedly feminist. Women face many uncertainties in the world today. Even in America, reproductive rights are slowly being stripped away, equal pay continues to be an issue, and trans women are belittled, denied basic freedoms, and even murdered on an almost daily basis. Feminism is a concept that is embraced in Witchcraft , which has long been considered a female-centric practice. This is not to say that men can not practice Witchcraft , they absolutely can, but there is an undeniable aspect of gender equality and female worship in many kinds of Witchcraft .

All of these factors have influenced young people to embrace Witchcraft , and while they are political, social, and economic, they are not any different from the reasons why people choose to practice more "traditional" or "established" religions or spiritualities. Belief systems are meant to provide comfort, nourish kindness and empathy, build community, and ignite passion. Witchcraft does all of these things in a way that makes sense to the rising gene

So You Want to Be a Witch

If you've decided to explore Witchcraft , you may benefit from asking yourself the following questions and answering honestly.

Exploring these questions will help you figure out what kind of Witch you are, how you like to practice, and who you can share your practice with.

- What drew you to Witchcraft ?

- What do you hope to gain from being a Witch?

- What makes you feel the most content? (Being in tune with nature, music, rituals, etc.)

- What do you want to be able to do with your Magick?

- What are your spiritual skills or desires? (Divination, psychic abilities, etc)

- Do you prefer to do your spiritual work alone or with others? Or both?

- Do you feel a particular affinity for certain aspects of nature? (The ocean, the moon, etc)
- Are you looking for a religion to practice from time to time or something that influences all aspect of your life?
- Are there certain deities or cultures you resonate with?
- What are your long-term spiritual goals?
- What are your values and ideals?
- What kind of person do you want to be?
- Who *are* you? Underneath all your roles and masks, who are you, really?

The Basics

(Tools, Methods, and General Information)

Energy

The practice of Witchcraft is based heavily off of the use and manipulation of energies. Everything has its own energies; rocks, waters, plants, objects, etc. Witches learn about, sense, and use these energies for their chosen purposes. Some objects have set energies while others can give off different energies at different times or can take on energies from outside sources.

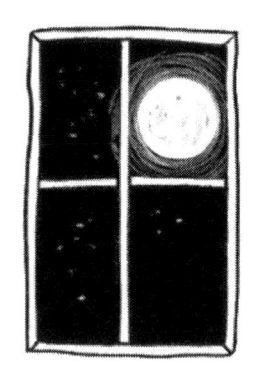

Humans are complicated when it comes to energy. They can create it, absorb it, release it, and change it. When it comes to spellcasting and ritual work, energies are focused through the intent of the Witch. Knowing how to properly work with energies is imperative to being a successful Witch.

Charging is the act of filling an object or substance with the energy of a source. The source is most often a person or a celestial being such as the moon, the sun, or a planet. A simple way to cleanse an object using a celestial body is to leave it in direct light from that celestial body. It is important to remove the item before the light disappears. For example, when charging a crystal in the moonlight, one should leave it on a windowsill where it can soak up moonlight, but it must be removed before the sun comes up so as not to charge it with conflicting energies.

Cleansing is a necessary practice that is used to expel any lingering energies from an object. Cleansing can be done through a variety of methods including smoke cleansing and water cleansing. Smoke cleansing can be done by burning an appropriate plant and engulfing the object within the smoke of it. The most popular plants to smoke cleanse with include Sage (although one should avoid using white sage as it is endangered), Rosemary, Cedar, and Lavender. Water cleansing requires the object to be submerged in a pure water, such as moon water, seawater, snow water, or rainwater. (Please note: it is not acceptable to refer to smoke cleansing as "smudging", as that term belongs to a closed culture).

Visualizing energies is an easy way to get used to feeling one's own energies and practice absorbing and releasing energy. A good way to start working with one's own energy is to assign it a color and then picture that energy moving from the chest, through the arm, and out from the tips of the fingers into an object or substance.

Energy plays a part in every aspect of Witchcraft and so all of the aforementioned techniques will be revisited and explained in greater detail later on in this guide.

Elements

The four basic elements of this planet; air, earth, fire, and water, each have a very important place in Witchcraft .

Air is an active element that has a connection to sound and the basics of life. It is correspondent with the direction of the East, where the sun rises. Air is often invoked in matters dealing with travel. Some of its common associations are:

- The color Yellow
- The Spring season
- Winged insects and avians
- Transparent stones
- The senses of hearing and smell
- Practices like divination and visualization.

Earth is the connector of all elements. It is heavy and passive, the opposite of Air. It is associated with the North and possesses qualities of darkness, quietness, and thickness or density. Earth's common correspondences are:

- Qualities like fertility, stability, and nurturing
- The color Green
- The Winter season
- Practices such as binding and gardening

Fire is arguably the element used most often in spells and rituals. It is an active element that is associated with the direction of the South and is strongly connected to cleansing. Fire is commonly associated with:

- The colors White and Orange
- The Summer season
- Qualities such as passion, rebirth, courage, cleansing, and destruction

Water has many uses within Witchcraft and comes in several different distinct forms. The origination of the water being used matters quite a bit as seawater has its own properties that differentiate it from rainwater or stream water. Water is generally associated with:

- The element Mercury
- The Moon and Venus
- Feminine energy
- Purification
- The color Blue

The following uses and correspondences are unique to specific types of water:

Creek and stream water: Purification and cleansing, promoting harmony

Dew: Matters of health, especially eyesight, beauty. Dew that is gathered at dawn on Beltane is considered the most powerful.

Fog and mists: Partnerships and balance.

Ice: Ice is most closely associated with transformation.

Pond or lake water: Waters that come from stagnant environments, like ponds or lakes, have associations with relaxation, peacefulness, and contentment.

Rainwater: Rainwater is often harvested to be used in cleansing ceremonies and is regarded as extremely pure and powerful.

River water: River water is used to help facilitate movement forward and healing from the past.

Seawater: Seawater is used to help manifest one's goals, reenergize, and cleanse.

Snow: Like ice, snow is a powerful tool for transformation. It also is used for cleansing.

Spring water: Spring water is used for protection.

Swamp and wastewater: Banishing and binding, often to deter negative influences.

Well water: Water from a well is associated with wishes, luck, and connection to one's intuition

Crystals

Crystals are one of the most common Witchcraft tools. Every crystal and stone type has its own inherent energies, correspondences, and uses. Every Witch eventually comes to rely on certain crystals that they feel a connection to. Correspondences are mainly decided through a combination of tradition and trial and error. Crystals can be used in a variety of ways. Crystals are often an ingredient in spells and rituals and are used as an energy source.

Leaving crystals in appropriate places around the home can fill your living space with the proper energies for you and your cohabitants. Placing a crystal for safe travel, such as Tigers Eye, in the glove compartment of a vehicle can help keep the passengers safe. Crystals can also be used as an anxiety relief tool during work or academic study when rubbed in one's hand during such activities.

Crystals are commonly used for self-care as well. Many religions and spiritual practices recognize the power of crystal healing. This can be accomplished through physical contact with the appropriate crystals, bathing with crystals (provided that they are not water soluble), and commonly sleeping with crystals under one's pillow.

General Crystal Correspondences

Agate: Strength, Courage, Longevity, Love, Healing, Protection.

Amazonite: Success, Self-Expression.

Amber: Luck, Love, Mental Clarity.

Amethyst: Dreams, Overcoming Addiction, Healing, Psychism, Peace, Love, Happiness.

Aquamarine: Psychic Awareness, Peace, Purification.

Aventurine: Mental Powers, Eyesight, Gambling, Money, Peace, Healing, Luck.

Azurite: Psychic Energy, Dreams, Divination, Healing, Concentration.

Beryl: Protection from Weather

Bloodstone: Healing from Surgery or Blood Illnesses, Victory, Courage, Wealth, Strength.

Blue Lace Agate: Overcoming Obstacles, Wishes.

Blue Stalactite: Life Direction, Finding a Personal Path, Self-Knowledge.

Calcite: Centering, Overcoming Fear, Grounding.

Carnelian (Orange/Red): Fertility, Creativity, Domestic Happiness, Banishment of Jealousy.

Celestite: Growth, Compassion, Verbal Skills

Chrysocolla (Blue/Green): Inner-Pcace, Wisdom.

Chrysophrase (Green): Clear Communication, Eloquence, Persuasiveness.

Citrine: Self-Esteem, Balance, Protection Against Nightmares.

Crazy Lace Agate: Latent Talents, Career Success.

Clear Quartz: Amplification of Energy, Cleansing, Can be used to enhance the powers of other crystals.

Diamond: Resilience, Perseverance, Tenacity.

Emerald: Protection, Prosperity, Memory, Learning.

Fluorite: Healing.

Garnet: Hope, Protection Against Rumors, Imagination.

Goldstone: Money, Commerce.

Hematite: Protection, Absorption of Negativity, Grief.

Iron Pyrite (Fool's Gold): Healing, addiction, strengthening of the will.

Jade: Serenity, Peace, Fortune.

Jasper: Openness, Flexibility.

Jet: Protection, Emotional Clarity, Mourning.

Kunzite: Communication, Relaxation, Balance, Creativity.

Lapis Lazuli: Truth, Spiritual Healing, Restful Sleep, Self Expression.

Lepidolite: Physical Strength, Nightmare Deflection, Peace.

Loadstone: Good Fortune, Money, Love, Fidelity.

Malachite: Success in Love and Business, Creativity, Fertility.

Merlinite: Connection to Intuition, Psychic Knowledge, Mediumship.

Meteorite: Connection to the Universe, Comfort in new Environments.

Moldavite: Connectivity, Ease of Doubts, Meditation.

Moonstone: Mystery, Realizations of Self, Psychic Protection, Deflection of Negativity, Healing from Emotional Trauma.

Mother-Of-Pearl: Emotional Commitment, Marriage, True Love.

Obsidian: Protection, Grounding,

Onyx: Spirit Contact, Rebirth, Past Life Regression, Protection.

Opal: Psychic Development, Openness, Sensitivity to Spirits Presence.

Peridot: Prosperity, Sleep, Emotional Balance, Intuition.

Pearl: Peace, Compassion, Positivity.

Rhodochrosite: Compassion, Sexual Chemistry, Fertility.

Rhodonite: Healing of Emotional Pain, Grief, Reconciliation.

Rose Quartz: Love, Happiness.

Ruby: Blood Circulation, Energy, Leadership, Protection from Nightmares.

Sapphire: Inspiration, Power, Protection.

Smokey Quartz: Altered States, Healing, Absorption of Energy.

Sodalite: Psychic Development, Clairvoyance.

Sunstone: Passion, Sexuality, Energy.

Sugilite: Dream Protection, Stress Reduction, Calmness.

Tigers Eye: Popularity, Persuasiveness, Communication, Safe Travels.

Tiger's Iron: Protection, Clarity of Knowledge, Vitality.

Topaz: Tranquility, Prosperity.

Tourmaline: Friendship, Peace, Sleep, Inspiration.

Turquoise: Psychic Openness, Consecration, Protection.

Zircon: Protection Against theft, Alertness, Emotional Balance.

Crystals by Elemental Correspondences

Earth: Green Agate, Moss Agate, Green Calcite, Cat's Eye, Coal, Emerald, Brown Jasper, Green Jasper, Jet, Kunzite, Malachite, Olivine, Peridot, Black Tourmaline, Green Tourmaline, Turquoise.

Air: Aventurine, Mottled Jasper, Mica, Pumice, Sphene.

Fire: Banded Agate, Black Agate, Red Agate, Amber, Apache Tears, Bloodstone, Carnelian, Citrine, Garnet, Hematite, Red Jasper, Obsidian, Pipestone, Ruby, Serpentine, Tiger's Eye, Topaz, Red Tourmaline, Zircon.

Water: Blue Lace Agate, Amethyst, Aquamarine, Azurite, Blue Calcite, Jade, Lapis Lazuli, Lepidolite, Moonstone, Pink Calcite, Celestite, Sapphire, Selenite, Sodalite, Sugilite, Blue Tourmaline, Pink Tourmaline.

Crystals by Associations

Astral Projection: Crystal Quartz, Opal.

Beauty: Amber, Cat's Eye, Jasper, Opal, Orange Zircon.

Business Success: Bloodstone, Malachite, Yellow Tourmaline, Yellow Zircon.

Centering: Calcite, Brown Zircon.

Childbirth: Sard, Pumice.

Courage: Agate, Amethyst, Aquamarine, Bloodstone, Carnelian, Diamond, Lapis Lazuli, Sardonyx, Tiger's Eye, Red Tourmaline, Turquoise.

Defense: Onyx, Sapphire.

Divination: Azurite, Flint, Hematite, Jet, Mica, Moonstone, Obsidian, Tiger's Eye.

Dreams: Amethyst, Azurite.

Friendship: Chrysoprase, Pink Tourmaline, Turquoise.

Grounding: Hematite, Kunzite, Moonstone, Obsidian, Black Tourmaline.

Happiness: Amethyst, Chrysoprase, Yellow Zircon.

Health and Healing: Agate, Amber, Amethyst, Azurite, Bloodstone, Calcite, Carnelian, Cat's Eye, Celestite, Crystal Quartz, Diamond, Flint, Garnet,

Hematite, Jade, Jasper, Jet, Lapis Lazuli, Peridot, Petrified Wood, Sapphire, Sodalite, Staurolite, Sugilite, Sunstone, Topaz, Red Zircon.

Love: Agate, Alexandrite, Amber, Amethyst, Calcite, Chrysocolla, Emerald, Jade, Lapis Lazuli, Lepidolite, Malachite, Moonstone, Olivine, Rhodochrosite, Sapphire, Sard, Topaz, Pink Tourmaline, Turquoise.

Luck: Alexandrite, Amber, Apache Tear, Chalcedony, Chrysoprase, Jet, Lepidolite, Olivine, Opal, Sardonyx, Tiger's Eye, Turquoise.

Magickal Powers: Bloodstone, Crystal Quartz, Malachite, Opal, Ruby.

Meditation: Sapphire, Sodalite.

Mental Power: Aventurine, Emerald, Fluorite, Sphene, Zircon.

Nightmares (To Quell): Citrine, Jet, Lepidolite, Ruby.

Peace: Amethyst, Aquamarine, Aventurine, Calcite, Carnelian, Kunzite, Lepidolite, Malachite, Obsidian, Rhodonite, Sardonyx, Sodalite, Blue Tourmaline.

Physical Energy: Calcite, Rhodochrosite, Selenite, Spinel, Sunstone, Tiger's eye, Red Tourmaline, Red Zircon.

Physical Strength: Agate, Amber, Bloodstone, Diamond, Garnet.

Protection: Agate, Amber, Apache Tears, Calcite, Carnelian, Cat's Eye, Citrine, Quartz Crystal, Jade, Jasper, Jet, Lapis Lazuli, Lepidolite, Malachite, Mica, Moonstone, Obsidian, Olivine, Onyx, Peridot, Serpentine, Sunstone, Tiger's Eye, Topaz, Clear Zircon.

Psychism: Amethyst, Aquamarine, Azurite, Citrine, Crystal Quartz, Emerald, Lapis Lazuli.

Purification: Aquamarine, Calcite.

Reconciliation: Diamond, Selenite.

Spirituality: Calcite, Diamond, Lepidolite, Sephene, Sugilite.

Sleep: Moonstone, Peridot, Blue Tourmaline.

Sexual Energy: Carnelian, Sunstone, Yellow Zircon.

Travel: Chalcedony, Dalmation Jasper, Orange Zircon.

Wisdom: Chrysocolla, Jade, Sodalite, Sugilite.

Wealth: Aventurine, Bloodstone, Calcite, Cat's Eye, Chrysoprase, Coal, Emerald, Jade, Olivine, Opal, Peridot, Ruby, Sapphire, Spinel, Staurolite, Tiger's Eye, Topaz, Green Tourmaline, Brown Zircon, Green Zircon

Herbs, Flowers, and Plants

Herbs and plants are arguably the most powerful and most often used tools in Witchcraft . They can be used in many different forms, but most are used in a dried state. Growing different plants is also a wonderful way to practice Witchcraft while also creating your own ingredients. Witches who work primarily with plants or through gardening, commonly known as "Green" Witches, use not only a plant's general attributes and correspondences but also detect and harness the individual energies of a herb or plant.

It is of the utmost importance to research the properties of an herb before using it in one's practice. Personal allergies and toxicity of a plant can pose an extreme threat to the Witch using it as well as any pets or roommates. Please note that many common fruits, such as apples, apricots, cherries, and peaches contain poisonous chemicals in their seeds.

* - Toxicity of specific plant parts and/or to certain living things*

A

Adam & Eve Roots: Love, Happiness.

Adder's Tongue: Healing.

African Violet: Spirituality, Protection.

Agaric: Fertility.

Agrimony: Restoration, Healing, Benevolence.

Ague Root: Protection

Alfalfa: Prosperity, Anti-Hunger, Money

Alkanet: Purification, Prosperity

Allspice: Money, Luck, Healing

Almond: Money, Prosperity, Wisdom

Aloe: Protection, Luck

Althea: Protection, Psychic Powers

Alyssum: Protection, Moderating Anger

Amaranth: Healing Heartbreak

Anemone*: Protection, Healing

Angelica: Shield from negativity, purification, temperance

Anise: Ward against evil and bad dreams

Arabic Gum: Spirituality, Enchantment, Protection, Platonic Love

Arnica Flower: Psychic powers

Arrow Root: Healing, Purification

Asafoetida: Banishing

Ash: Protection, Luck, Prosperity

Aspen: Eloquence, Clairvoyance

Aster: Love

Avens: Purification

Azalea*: Happiness, Young Love, Light Spirits

B

Baby's Breath*: Innocence

Bachelor Button: Love

Balm, Lemon: Love, Success, Healing

Balm of Gilead: Healing From Grief, Relief From Stress, Mending a Broken Heart

Balmony: Patience, Tenacity, Perseverance

Balsam Fir: Strength, Insight

Bamboo: Hex Breaking, Luck, Wishes

Banyan: Luck, Happiness

Barberry: Cleansing, Independence, Atonement

Barley: Love, Healing, Protection

Basil: Wealth, Sympathy, Protection

Bat's Head Root: Wish Granting

Bay Laurel: Purification, Cleansing

Bay Leaf: Fortune, Success, Healing

Beech: Wishes, Happiness

Belladonna*: Astral Projection, Healing From Past Loves, Protection

Benzoin: Purification, Prosperity

Bergamot: Money, Success, Prosperity

Betony Flower: Protection, Binding

Birch: Protection, Purification

Birds of Paradise*: Freedom, Faithfulness

Bistort: Psychic Powers, Fertility

Bittersweet: Protection, Healing

Blackberry: Healing, Money, Protection

Black Haw: Luck, Power, Employment

Black Pepper: Banishing, Protection

Black Walnut: Divine Energy, Blessing

Bladderwrack: Protection, Sea Spells, Wind Spells, Financial Success

Bleeding Heart: Unrequited Love

Bloodroot: Love, Protection, Purification

Bluebell: Truth, Friendship, Comfort, Mourning

Blue Flag: Prosperity, Money

Boneset: Safe Travel, Healing

Borage: Tranquility, Courage

Brazil Nut: Love

Broom: Divination, Purification

Buchu: Psychic Powers, Prophetic Dreams

Buckeye: Luck, Wealth

Buckthorn*: Luck In Legal Matters

Buckwheat: Protection, Riches, Wealth

Buttercup*: Neatness, Childishness, Innocence

C

Cactus: Banishing, Protection

Calamint: Emotional Recovery

Calamus: Luck, Healing, Money, Protection

Calendula: Comfort, Strength

Calla Lily*: Beauty

Camellia: Wealth

Camphor*: Dreaming, Divination, Psychic Abilities

Caper: Potency, Lust

Caraway: Preventing Loved Ones From Departure

Cardamom: Lust, Love, Fidelity

Carnation*: Joy, Devotion, Balance

Carob: Protection, Health

Cascara Sagrada: Legal Matters, Money, Protection Against Evil

Cashew: Money

Castor*: Protection

Catnip: Cat Magic, Love

Cat Tail: Lust

Cayenne: Severing Emotional Ties

Cedar: Confidence, Strength, Power

Celandine: Fighting Depression, Self-Confidence

Chamomile: Stress Reduction, Restful Sleep

Chestnut: Love

Chia: Health

Chickweed: Fertility, Love

Chicory: Removing Obstacles

Chili Pepper: Fidelity, Hex Breaking, Love

Chinaberry: Luck

Chrysanthemum*: Cheerfulness, Abundance, Optimism

Cilantro: Domestic Peace

Cinnamon: Spirituality, Success, Healing, Power,

Cinquefoil: Love, Money, Health, Power, Wisdom, Memory, Self-Confidence

Citronella: Eloquence, Persuasiveness, Prosperity.

Clove: Protection, Love, Money

Coffee: Protection Against Negative Thoughts, Peace of Mind

Coltsfoot: Peace, Tranquility

Columbine: Courage, Love

Comfrey: Safe Travel, Stability, Endurance

Coriander: Health, Protection, Longevity

Cornflower: Harmony

Cowslip: Concentration, Focus

Coxcomb: Protection

Crocus: Happiness, Joy

Crowfoot: Love, Marriage, Commitment

Culver's Root: Purification

Cumin: Theft Prevention, Protection

Curry: Protection

Cyclamen: Fertility, Lust, Happiness

Cypress: Mourning, Emotional Healing

D

Daffodil*: Love, Fertility, Luck

Dahlia: Dignity, Elegance

Daisy: Purity, Beauty, Innocence

Damiana: Lust, Sex

Dandelion Leaf: Spirit Communication, Healing, Banishing Negativity

Dandelion Root: Divination, Sleep Magick

Datura:** Hex Breaking, Sleep, Protection

Day Lily: Devotion

Deer's Tongue: Physical Attraction, Psychic Powers

Delphinium (Larkspur): Protection In Battle

Devil's Bit: Love, Protection, Lust

Devil's Claw: Protection, Ward Against Unwanted Company

35

Devil's Shoestring: Luck, Employment

Dill: Protection, Money, Lust, Luck

Dodder: Love, Divination,

Dogbane*: Deception, Romance

Dogwood: Protection, Health, Confidence

Dragon's Blood: Protection, Energy, Purification

Dulse: Lust, Domestic Harmony

E

Ebony: Protection, Power

Echinacea: Strengthening Spells

Edelweiss: Courage, Nobility

Elder: Counteracting Enchantments, House Blessing, Protection

Elecampane: Protection Against Violence

Elm: Love

Endive: Lust, Love

Eucalyptus*: Healing, Protection

Evening Primrose: Attraction, Love, Inner Beauty

Eyebright: Mental Powers, Psychic Power

F

Fennel: Strength, Vitality, Virility

Fenugreek: Money, Fertility

Fern: Mental Clarity, Concentration

Feverfew: Protection Against Sickness

Figwort: Home Blessing

Flax: Healing, Home Protection, Wealth

Fleabane: Chastity, Protection

Forget Me Not: True Love, Memories

Foxglove*: Spirit Communication, Home Protection, Vision

Frankincense: Cleansing, Consecration, Meditation

Fuchsia: Amiability

Fumitory: Spirit Connection, Home Consecration

G

Galangal: Wealth, Legal Success

Gardenia: Peace, Comfort

Gardenia: Refinement, Purity, Secret Love

Gentian: Strength, Power

Geranium: Banishing Negative Thoughts, Happiness, Joy

Ginger: Sensuality, Sexuality, Prosperity

Ginkgo Biloba: Fertility, Healing

Ginseng: Love, Beauty, Lust

Gladiolus: Preparedness, Beauty, Love At First Sight

Globe Amaranth: Enduring Love

Goats Rue: Healing, Health

Goldenrod: Money, Success

Goldenseal: Business Success

Golden Seal: Healing, Money

Goosegrass: Wisdom, Tenacity

Gorse: Love, Romance, Marraige

Gotu Kola: Meditation

Grains of Paradise: Luck, Employment, Power

Grape Seed: Fertility, Fruitfulness

Gravel Root: Employment, Harmony

Ground Ivy: Divination

Groundsel: Health, Healing

Guinea Pepper: Hexing

Gum Arabic: Protection, Enchantment, Friendship

H

Hawthorn: Fertility, Chastity, Happiness, Rebirth

Hazel: Luck, Fertility, Anti-Lightning, Protection, Wishes

Heather*: Protection, Longevity, Luck

Heliotrope: Cheerfulness, Prosperity

Hemlock*: Cursing

Hemp: Healing, Love, Vision, Meditation

Henbane*: Love, Attraction, Consecration

Henna: Healing, Love, Warding

Hibiscus: Divination, Dreams

Hickory: Legal Matters, Protection

High John the Conqueror: Strength, Confidence, Success

Holly*: Marriage, Love, Luck

Honeysuckle: Money, Success, Abundance

Hops: Peaceful Sleep, Serenity

Horehound: Mental Clarity, Creativity, Inspiration

Horseradish: Purification

Horseshoe Chestnut: Money, Healing

Horsetail: Healing, Cleansing

Houndstongue: Dreams

Houseleek: Luck, Protection, Love

Huckleberry: Luck, Protection, Dream Magick

Hyacinth*: Peace Of Mind, Restful Sleep, Good Fortune

Hydrangea*: Hex Breaking, Binding

Hyssop: Purification, Cleansing

I

Impatiens: Maternal Love

Indigo Weed: Protection

Iris*: Wisdom, Courage, Faith

Irish Moss: Luck

Ivy*: Fertility, Love, Positivity

J

Jasmine: Divination, Charging, Soul Mate Attraction

Jezebel Root: Money, Success

Job's Tears: Wishes, Blessing, Luck, Wealth

Juniper*: Good Health, Potency

K

Kava-Kave: Sex, Astral Work

Knotweed: Binding, Cursing

Kola Nut: Peace, Calming

L

Lady's Mantle: Beauty, Sex, Love

Lady's Slipper: Protection

Larch: Protection, Anti-Theft

Laurel: Marriage, Love, Protection

Lavender: Love, Protection, Sleep, Chastity

Leek: Love

Lemon Balm: Success, Psychic Development

Lemon Grass: Psychic Cleansing

Lemon Verbena: Ward Against Nightmares

Licorice: Love, Lust, Fidelity

Lilac: Wisdom, Luck, Memory

Lily: Fertility, Renewal

Lily of the Valley: Peace, Tranquility

Linden: Love, Restful Sleep

Liverwort: Protection, Love, Longevity

Lobelia: Love

Loosestrife: Peace, Protection

Lotus: Psychic Openness, Spiritual Growth

Lovage: Purification, Premonitions, Psychic Cleansing

Lucky Hand: Good Luck, Protection, Safe Travel

Lungwort: Safe Air Travel

M

Mace: Concentration, Focus, Self Discipline

Magnolia: Fidelity, Love

Maidenhair: Beauty, Love

Mandrake: Protection, Prosperity, Fruitfulness

Maple: Wealth, Longevity, Luck

Marigold*: Respect, Admiration, Luck

Marjoram: Cleansing, Purification

Marshmallow Root: Protection, Psychic Power

Masterwort: Strength, Courage, Protection

Meadowsweet: Employment

Mesquite: Healing

Mimosa: Protection, Love, Dream Magick

Mint: Communication, Vitality

Mistletoe*: Fertility, Creativity

Molukka: Protection

Monk's Hood*: Protection

Moonwort: Prosperity

Morning Glory*: Binding, Banishing

Motherwort: Confidence, Success

Mugwort: Lust, Fertility

Mulberry: Protection, Strength

Mullein: Protection From Negative Magick

Musk: Self-Esteem

Mustard Seed: Courage, Faith, Endurance

Myrrh: Meditation, Healing

Myrtle*: Love, Fertility, Youth

N

Narcissus: Vanity, Self-Esteem

Nasturtium: Achievement, Aspiration

Neroli: Joy, Happiness

Nettle: Dispelling Fear, Strengthening Will, Protection

Nutmeg: Money, Prosperity, Luck

O

Oak: Purification, Fertility

Oak Moss: Luck, Money

Oats: Prosperity

Oleander*: Love, Protection

Olive Leaf: Peace, Potency, List

Orange Blossom: Wealth, Stability

Orchid: Concentration, Will Power

Oregano: Joy, Vitality, Energy

Orris Root: Popularity, Persuasiveness

42

Osha Root: Protection

P

Palm: Fertility, Potency

Pansy*: Love, Divination

Paprika: Energy, Cursing

Papyrus: Protection

Parsley: Domestic Harmony and Protection

Parsnip: Sex

Passion Flower: Friendship, prosperity

Patchouli: Money, Love

Peat Moss: Home Protection

Pecan: Money, Employment

Pennyroyal*: Tranquility, Peace

Peony: Good Fortune, Business success

Pepper: Banishing Negativity

Peppermint: Healing, Purification

Periwinkle*: Domestic Stability

Petunia: Beauty, Joy

Pimento: Love

Pimpernel: Protection

Pine: Rebirth, Renewal, New Beginnings

Pink Root: Healing

Pistachio: Counteracting Love Spells

Pleurisy Root: Healing

Plumeria: Persuasiveness, Eloquence

Poinsettia*: Celebration

Poke Root*: Breaking Hexes, Courage

Poppy: Fertility, Prosperity, Love
Primrose: Resolution, Revealing Secrets, Works Against Dishonesty

Pussy Willow: Maternal Love, Enchantment

Q

Quassia: Love

Quince: Happiness, Luck, Protection

R

Radish: Protection, Lust

Ragwort: Protection

Red Clover: Fidelity, Love

Rhododendron: Alertness, Caution

Rhubarb*: Protection, Fidelity

Rice: Fertility, Money

Rose: Divine Love, Domestic Happiness, Friendship

Rose Geranium: Dispels Gossip

Rose Hips: Healing, Luck

Rosemary: Good Health, Love, Memory, Sleep

Rowan: Success, Banishment

Rue: Mental Healing, Freedom, Protection

Rye: Love, Fidelity, Self-Control

S

Safflower: Sex, Cursing

Saffron: Love, Sex, Lust

Sage: Purification, Recovery From Grief, Mental Stability, Wisdom

Saltpeter: Fidelity

Sandalwood: Cleansing, Protection

Sanicle: Safe Travel

Sarsaparilla: Vitality, Health, Sex

Sassafras: Overcoming Addiction

Savory: Sex, Passion

Scullcap: Fidelity, Harmony

Sea Salt: Cleansing, Grounding, Purification

Senna: Lust, Love

Sesame: Passion, Lust

Shallot: Luck

Shamrock: Good Fortune, Luck

Sheep Sorrel: Healing From Illness

Skunk Cabbage: Legal Matters

Slippery Elm: Protection

Snakeroot, Black: Strength, Protection

Snapdragon: Protection, Purification

Solomon's Seal Root: Cleansing, Binding

Sow Thistle: Strength, Stamina

Spanish Moss: Protection

Spearmint: Healing, Love, Sleep Protection

Spiderwort: Love

Spikenard: Luck, Health

Squaw Vine: Fertility

Squill Root: Prosperity, Financial Stability

St. John's Wort: Health, Sickness Prevention,

Banishing, Protection

Star Anise: Psychic Awareness

Sugar: Love, Sex, Lust

Sunflower: Energy, Power, Wisdom

Sweetgrass: Peace, Unity

Sweet Pea*: Loyalty

T

Tamarind: Love

Tansy: Health, Longevity

Tansy: Longevity, Protection

Tarragon: Compassion, Consecration

Tea Tree: Harmony

Thistle: Protection, Healing

Thyme: Loyalty, Affection, Social Success

Toadflax: Protection, Hex Breaking

Toadstool: Rain Making

Tobacco*: Peace, Confidence, Strength

Tulip*: Desire, Relationships

Turmeric: Healing

Turnip: Ending Relationships

U

Urva Ursi: Strengthening Psychic Powers

V

Valerian: Dream Magick, Reconciliation

Vanilla: Love, Passion

Venus Flytrap: Protection, Love

Vervain: Purification, Money, Peace

Vetch: Fidelity

Vetivert: Money, Prosperity

Vinegar: Banishing, Binding

Violet: Calming, Prophetic Visions, Creativity

W

Walnut: Blessing

Watercress: Sex

Wheat: Fertility

Willow: Lunar Magick, Strength, Healing

Wintergreen: Good Luck

Wisteria*: Victory, Psychic Openness

Witch Hazel: Protection, Chastity

Witch's Burr: Power, Goodness

Wolf's Bane*: Protection

Wood Aloe: Consecration, Prosperity

Wood Betony: Protection From Nightmares

Woodruff: Victory, Protection, Money

Wormwood*: Quelling Anger, Protection From Violence

XYZ

Yarrow*: Divination, Love, Banishment, Marriage

Yerba Mate: Fidelity, Lust

Yerba Santa: Psychic Powers, Protection, Beauty

Yew*: Necromancy, Protection, Warding

Ylang Ylang: Sex, Love, Relaxation

Yohimbe Bark: Virility, Fertility, Lust

Yucca: Protection, Purification

Zinnia: Fortitude, Courage

Fruit, Vegetables, and Food Magick

Food Magick is the main aspect of Kitchen Witchcraft , but Witches of all kinds practice it, especially when celebrating the Sabbats or making offerings. Edible fruits and vegetable each have their own Magickal properties and uses in Witchcraft .

Certain foods, especially fruits, have strong roots in folklore and mythology that lend them special reverence in the Witchcraft world. For example, stemming from Greek mythology, pomegranates are associated with Persephone, the Queen of the Underworld.

The act of cooking or baking itself is akin to other practices, such as mixing potions or making sachets (more on that later). Combining ingredients to make something new is a Magickal process that imparts energy and intention into the product.

A

Apple: Emotional Healing, Love
Apricot: Love, Releasing Tension, Quelling Anxiety
Avocado: Beauty, Lust

B

Banana: Prevention Of Harm, Protection, Safe Travel
Bean: Ward Against Negativity
Beets: Love, Blood Substitution
Blackberry: Home Protection
Blueberry: Psychic Protection, Warding

C

Carrot: Fertility, Potency, Lust
Celery: Concentration, Sleep, Psychic Abilities
Cherry: Love, Blood Substitution
Chocolate: Virility, Love, Romance
Coconut: Home Protection, Property Protection
Corn: Fertility, Childbirth, Infant Protection

Cucumber: Fertility, Lust

F

Fig: Fertility, Sleep, Safe Travel, Home Protection

G

Grape: Wealth

L

Lemon: Purification, Cleansing, Friendship, Fidelity
Lettuce: Protection, Sleep, Chastity
Lime: Healing, Psychic Protection

O

Olive: Peace, Healing
Onion: Home Protection, Absorption Of Negativity, Banishment
Orange: Marriage, Beauty, Love

P

Pea: Wealth, Fortune
Peach: Wisdom, Warding
Pear: Love, Lust
Pineapple: Luck, Wealth
Plum: Protection, Love
Pomegranate: Fertility, Wishes, Blood Substitution
Potato: Warding Against Illness

R

Raspberry: Pregnancy, Childbirth

T

Tomato: Prosperity, Love, Protection

X,Y,Z

Zucchini: Love, Lust, Sex

Color Correspondences

Colors have their own attributes and associations, just like crystals and herbs do. Knowledge of these attributes can be used when picking ingredients or tools to accomplish a goal. Color Magick is often used when choosing candles for spells or rituals. Colors often have connections to different elements and can influence emotions.

Red: The color red is associated with fire, passion, courage, power, motivation, desire, and ambition.

Pink: Pink is associated with self-love, harmony, friendship, partnership, romance, and success

Orange: Like red, Orange is associated with the element of fire. It also corresponds to opportunities, happiness, alertness, kindness, strength, and dominance

Yellow: The color yellow is associated with the element of air, healing, productivity, creativity, prosperity, self-esteem, and intellect.

Green: Green has long been known as the color of life. It is associated with the element of earth, trust, healing and wellness, transformation, money, hope, rebirth, fertility, luck, and grace.

Blue: The color blue is understandably associated with the element of water as well as patience, peace, truth, loyalty, fidelity, travel, and calming.

Purple: Violet and purple are associated with clairvoyance, spiritual protection, wisdom, justice, memory, education, and kinship.

White: White corresponds with safety, enlightenment, and magnification.

Black: Black is used to represent or attract balance, creation, patience, stability, death, truth, and sacrifice.

Brown: The color brown is associated with the earth, security, nature, generosity, endurance, and grounding.

Animal Correspondences

Images, drawings, and humanely harvested pieces of animals (such as snake skin) are used in spells and rituals. It is important to remember that Animals are, generally, best left in their natural environments and should never be harmed for the sake of Witchcraft or other practices.

Ants - Patience, stamina, planning, perseverance, organization, self-discipline, teamwork, energy, and patience.

Armadillo - Trust, peace, pacifism, complexity, sensitivity, curiosity, introspection, protection.

Badgers - Determination, eagerness, strong will, focus, strategy, defense, independence, confidence.

Bats - Rebirth, accessing past lives, new ideas, transition, initiation, changes for the better, moon magic, understanding grief, and the ability to observe unseen.

Bears - Introspection, healing and inner knowledge, wisdom, defense, revenge, change, death and rebirth, communication with spirit, solitude, power, mother cunning, healer, gentle strength, transformation, astral travel, strength, unconscious mind, grounding, inner energy of the soul, earth magic, and facing fears.

Beavers - Building, gathering, persistence, shaping, and structure.

Bees - Female warrior energy, reincarnation, communication with the dead, service, gathering, community, connection to the Goddess Diana, helping earth-bound spirits move on to their proper place, concentration, and prosperity.

Birds - Associated with death and transitions, unity, freedom, and individuality.

Bobcats - Awareness, cunning, intellect, patience, playfulness.

Buffalo - Gratitude, abundance, consistency, strength, stability, blessing, prosperity.

Bulls - Virility, strength, stamina, confidence, fertility, determination.

Butterflies/Caterpillars - Transformation, reincarnation, balance, grace.

Camels - Endurance, transport, survival, conservation, adaptivity, obedience, temperance, humility.

Cats - Wholeness, guardians, independence, seeing the unseen, cleverness, a balancing of energies, moon magic, mystic powers, grace, understanding mystery, cleansing, and purification.

Cheetahs - Speed, passion, progress, assertion, evolution, perception, opportunity.

Chickens - Power of voice, language, seeking answers, sunrise Magick, Protection of family and community, Hearing your inner voice.

Chipmunks - Gathering, mobility, frugal living, and the ability to see both light and shadow.

Cows - Economy, connection to the earth, wealth and prosperity, and patience.

Coyote - Skill, instinct, transformation, inventiveness, intelligence, resourcefulness.

Deer - Gentleness, body awareness, kindness, gracefulness, sensitivity, peace, unconditional love, alertness, recognition of outside influences, innocence and earth magic.

Dogs - Family, wisdom, loyalty, protection, companionship, faithfulness, warnings, and earth and moon magic.

Donkeys - Stubbornness, ability to make decisions, intuition.

Ducks - Water energy and logic.

Elephants - Reliability, dignity, power, royalty, pride.

Elks - Stamina, strength, pride, power, majesty, agility, freedom, and nobility.

Ferrets - Information, seeing truth behind the facade.

Fish - Abundance, fertility, children, harmony, regeneration, love, and mind/emotion balance.

Foxes - Elusiveness, cleverness, feminine courage, subtlety, discretion, agility, cunning, slyness, fire magic, and intelligence.

Frogs - Healing, transformation, cleansing, understanding emotions, and connection with the element of water.

Giraffes - Vision, beauty, mystery, patience, elegance, cleverness, discernment, cooperation, gracefulness, gentleness.

Goats - Independence, confidence, tenacity, diligence, flexibility, healing and sun magic, abundance, and agility.

Gorillas - Communication, loyalty, leadership, compassion, intelligence, nobility, responsibility, nurturing, connectivity.

Hedgehogs - Energy, vitality, uniqueness, resourcefulness.

Hippopotami - Emotion, assertiveness, diversity, greatness, expressiveness, creativity, territory, supportive.

Horses - Power, stability and courage, Astral travel, protection, freedom, power, travel, and earth and moon magic.

Koala - Memory, pleasure, Magick, calming, trust.

Lion - Wisdom, power, royalty, dignity, courage, justice, ferocity, dominion, authority.

Mice - Scrutiny, innocence, faith, trust, shyness, quietness, details, and earth magic.

Monkeys - Honor, instinct, community, swiftness, good luck, playfulness, wildness, intelligence, action.

Moose - Agility, gentleness, solitude, visions, sensitivity, adaptability, discernment.

Otters - Joy, curiosity, dexterity, friendship, creativity.

Owls - Deception, wisdom, truth, patience, insight, darkness, and air magic.

Pigs - Truth, earth Magick, past life knowledge, intelligence, and cunning.

Polar Bears - Skill, Magick, strategy, isolation, transition, extremes, humanity, vigilance, independence, motherhood, determination, contemplation.

Pumas - Action, strength, nobility, patience, silence, decisions, leadership, guardianship, self-assurance.

Rabbits - Fear, faith, alertness, nurturing, conquering fear, safety, innocence, fertility, movement, sensitivity, luck, and moon magic.

Rams - Power, force, drive, energy, virility, protection, fearlessness.

Rats - Abundant reproduction, shrewdness, adaptability, success, social, restlessness, earth magic, stealth, and defense.

Reindeer - Travel, surety, service, guidance, sensitivity, exploration, opportunity.

Rhinoceroses - Achievement, heightened senses, inner resources, self-reliance.

Sheep - Balance, confidence, fertility, courage, new beginnings, abundance, and assurance.

Skunks - Defense, prudence, confidence, awareness, pacification, effectiveness, good judgment.

Snails - Perseverance and Determination.

Snakes - Transmutation, primitive or elemental energy, power, sexual potency. sensuality, shrewdness, and transformation.

Spiders - Shape-shifting, wisdom, creativity, divine inspiration, fate, illusion, feminine energy, and industry.

Squirrels - Discovery, change, trust, resourcefulness, balance in giving and receiving, awareness, sociability, playfulness, preparation, activity, energy, and earth magic.

Wolverines - Power, attitude, courage, war, defense, confidence, uncompromising, determination, resourcefulness.

Wolves - Wisdom, protection, shadow work, guidance, instinct, intelligence, success, perseverance, stability, loyalty, independence, spirit, freedom, guardianship, and earth and moon magic.

Zebras - Freedom, wildness, social, willful, durable, adaptable, determination, community

Spellcasting

Spellcasting is an essential part of Witchcraft . There are several extremely important methods and aspects to spellcasting that every Witch should know. These include circle casting, actions associations, sigil making and usage, sachet spells, and potion making. Spells themselves can be defined as a ritual or specific set of actions that invoke Magick to accomplish a certain goal.

Just as each herb and crystal has certain properties and strength, so do actions taken during rituals and spells. When writing spells it is important to include the proper actions to make sure your spell is as effective as possible.

Burning - Burning an object is a common practice in spells and rituals. Fire is considered a cleansing and activating force.

- If you want to destroy something's influence, burn it and dispose of the ashes away from your home.
- If you want to set something into motion, burn objects related to the situation to ash.

- If you want to activate certain energies, burn objects related to those involved.
- If you are performing a curse or hex, burn the object in the flame of a candle.

Burying/Abandoning - A Witch might bury an object for many reasons. They might want to put something to rest, perform a slow spell, or banish something. There are different ways in which one can bury an object to accomplish a desired outcome:

- If you want to keep something close, bury the object in your backyard.
- If you want to attract something, bury the object under the front doorstep
- If you want to disperse something to a distance, throw the object into a crossroads
- If you want to fix an influence, inter the object in a five-spot pattern
- If you want something to work by means of spirits, bury the object in a graveyard (but don't disrupt those buried there!)
- If you want to hide something's point of origin, conceal the object in a tree
- If you want something/someone to work by stealth, hide the object in clothing or on objects
- If you want an influence to begin or strengthen, throw the object East
- If you want an influence to end or weaken, throw the object West

Rubbing - Rubbing an object can be the easiest and most immediate way to experience Witchcraft . Transferring and garnering energy from objects can be done through physical contact with an object.

- If you want to put energy into an object, rub it with your left hand
- If you want to gather energy from an object, rub it with your right hand
- If you want to bring positivity, rub clockwise
- If you want to bring negativity, rub counterclockwise
- If you want to use crystals to heal, rub the appropriate stone on the affected part of the body.

Soaking - Water is one of the main elements used in Witchcraft . It comes in many forms with many different properties and uses.

- If you want something to move away and sink, throw it in running water
- If you want something's influence to rise and fall cyclically, float it in a tidal estuary
- If you want to protect or cleanse something, soak an object in rainwater
- If you are focused on your personal goals, soak your object in seawater
- If you want to bring about transformation, soak your object in snow/melted snow
- If you're trying to make a wish come true, soak your object in well water

- If you want to banish, soak your object in harbor water

Symbols

The **Pentagram** is one of the most recognizable symbols in the occult world. Pentagrams are five-pointed stars that are connected by a continuous line in 5 straight segments. The points of a Pentagram represent five elements, with the northern point being the non-physical element of spirit, followed clockwise by water, fire, earth, and air.

A **Pentacle** is a Pentagram that is surrounded by a circle. The circle in this symbol represents protection, infinity, and the cycle of life.

The **Goddess** symbol is one that is often seen in Witchcraft literature and fashion. It consists of a circle with two outward facing crescent moons on either side. Also called a **Triple Moon**, it represents the Maiden, the Mother, and the Crone and is a powerful feminist symbol that is associated with feminine energy and psychic abilities.

Tools

There are several traditional tools that Witches are known for utilizing during spellcasting and rituals. These items have specific uses in divination or representation and can often provide the main energy for a spell.

Athame (Ritual Knife) - Associated with Fire and the South, athames are used in a variety of rituals. It directs energy and creates magical circles.

Butterfly Wings - Some believe that butterfly wings can be representative of a Witch's soul.

Chalice - Representative of the female principle of Water. Can be used to represent fertility and spring.

Crystals - All crystals have specific energies and properties to aid in spells and rituals.

Crystal Ball - The use of crystal balls are common when images are required to relay information in divination.

Feathers - Representative of Air. Traditionally feathers are used as a sign of the spiritual plane and those who can connect to it.

Graveyard Dirt - Used as a link between the physical world and the next. Graveyard Work can be used in protection spells as well as curses. Some use Graveyard Dirt to communicate with restless spirits, such as those who were murdered or unjustly killed.

Pendulum - A pendulum is a weight at the end of a chain or string that is used for divination. The weight can be a stone, crystal, ring, coin, or pendant.

Skulls (Animal or otherwise) - Not only is the skull a Memento Mori, it also serves as a representative of the fragility of the physical form. Some believe that skulls are a housing place for spirits, not only those of the former owners', but for lost souls as well.

Snake Skin - Represents transformation and growth as well as new opportunities. Snake Skin can boost the effectiveness of certain spells, including protection spells and energy cleansing.

Stones/Rocks - Much like crystals, all stones have different properties depending on what kind of rock they are and even where they came from. Some stones hold energies that they have come in contact with. These energies should not be underestimated.

Tarot Cards - Form of divination that channels the energy of the subject to report information about that person's past/present/future.

Spell Types

There are many different ways to accomplish goals in Witchcraft . These terms each define a type of ritual and the circumstances that they best serve.

Banishing is the act of driving away unwanted entities, energies, or situations. Many rituals include a banishing section to help ensure that no negative influences can be released from an invocation.

Binding is similar to banishing but is used for disarming or restricting a subject. Binding can be done to objects that a Witch does not want to use as well as entities or people who wish to do them harm. There are many instances in which binding can be an appropriate and useful form of spellcasting.

Enchantment is used when infusing energy or intent into an object. Objects that are enchanted are often referred to as "charms". Items can be enchanted using several different methods of energy transfer.

Green spells are those that focus on matters of luck, wealth and finances, and success.

Love spells are a topic of debate in the Witchcraft community. The role of consent in romantic or relationship-focused Magick is important but often overlooked. The age-old notion of a potion or ritual to make one person fall in love with another without one party's knowledge is a violation of the unknowing person's free will and is, therefore, morally wrong.

Negative Magick, formerly known as "black Magick" (though this is an outdated term) is a name given to spells and rituals that are intended to harm another. There are several types of negative spells including:

- **Curses**: a type of spell most often performed to cause serious and/or permanent hard to the target.

- **Hexes:** a ritual designed to cause the target harm. The main difference between a Hex and a Curse is that a Hex is broken or finished when the target learns their lesson or realizes their wrongdoing.

- **Jinxes**: a spell used to bring small misfortunes or bad luck to the target. Jinxes are usually temporary and can be heavily tied to the personal superstitions of the target.

On the opposite end of the spectrum from negative Magick, **White Magick** focuses mainly on protection, cleansing, and healing. It is often done with the intention of helping people or beings that are not the practitioner themselves.

Sigils are symbols created to be charged with a certain intent. They can be worn, burned, buried, and used in spells. These symbols often have characteristics based on numerology and astrology, but they are not required to.

Warding can be an imperative act in Witchcraft . It is the process of creating a space that is protected or safe. These spaces can range from ritual locations to one's home to a single object.

Circle Casting is a form of Warding. Casting a circle is done when creating a sacred space in which to perform Magick. This circle may be cast by solitary practitioners or groups. To cast a circle, one must first make sure to cleanse themselves in order to prevent unwanted energies from being brought into the circle. The area in which the circle will be cast must then be cleansed as well. Next, the four directions should be marked on the outskirts of the circle using candles or other markers. Many Witches choose to use salt to physically outline the circle. The salt acts as a protection border.

Sachets, Potions, and Jar Spells

Spells come in many different forms. One form is that of the **sachet spell**. Sachets are small pieces of material that are filled with ingredients and then tied closed. The color of the material, as well as the material itself, is important when creating a sachet spell. The items inside of a sachet are very important and choosing the correct ingredients can determine how effective your sachet is. These Magickal objects are usually kept on one's person or placed in order to facilitate the spell. For example, a sachet for restful sleep may be tied to a bedpost.

Jar spells, also known as bottle spells, are used mainly for long-term Witchcraft . These jars are filled with the proper ingredients and then sealed with wax and buried or kept in order to break hexes, bring many years of love, peace, employment, or protection.

Potions are mixtures of ingredients (mainly liquid) that are oftentimes enchanted or infused with energy to add to the strength of the elixir. There are several different kinds of potions including suspensions, which contain non-dissolving particles as well as edible brews like tea.

Moon Phases, Times, and Days of the Week

When casting spells or performing rituals, timing can be crucial. Factors such as the phase of the moon, the time of day, and even the day of the week can influence the effectiveness of a spell. By knowing when the best time to perform a spell is, one can ensure that their work is done at an optimal time.

Moon Phases

The days of a **new moon** are great times to perform spells that are meant to facilitate new ventures, new relationships, job success, and health.

A **waxing moon** is an appropriate time to perform Magick that promotes courage, wealth, and success.

A **full moon** can bring extreme energy shifts and some Witches may find that their sleep is either hindered or helped by its presence. During a full moon rituals and spells pertaining to protection, divination, and prophecy should be performed.

A **waning moon** brings with it an opportunity to enhance banishing rituals as well as spells to get rid of illness and negativity.

Dark moons are wonderful times to focus on removing negative influences in one's life and protecting oneself against attackers.

Days of The Week

Sunday is a day to deal with matters of success, wealth, and prosperity.

Monday is an ideal day to cast spells that have to do with sleep, peace, beauty, fertility, and wisdom.

Tuesday is for spells to bring courage, victory, success, strength, defense, and conviction.

Wednesday can enhance spells that deal with communication, change, luck, and creativity.

Thursday is a good day for spells to bring abundance, prosperity, and healing.

Fridays are optimal times for romance, passion, and love spells.

Saturday is a day to perform banishment, protection, and cleansing rituals.

Significant Times of Day

Midnight is a popular spellcasting time. Long considered the "Witching hour", Midnight is significant because it marks the changing of one day to the next. Some believe that this is when the veil between our world and the spirit world is thinnest over the course of a day.

3 a.m. has religious and cultural symbolism, especially in Christianity. Known as the "Devil's Hour", some believe that this is the time at which demonic entities are the strongest in the human world.

4 a.m. is considered a time of luck and victory.

8 a.m. is a time to work on personal change

10 a.m. is an ideal hour to focus on resolutions and goals

2 p.m. is a time to use Magick to enhance relationships and love

4 p.m. is considered a time of harmony between the elements

9 p.m. can be a great time for introspection

10 p.m. may be a time of clear-mindedness

Divination

Divination is the practice of using tools or methods to gain knowledge or make contact with outside forces and energies. There are many ways to use divination.

Astrology is a form of popular divination that uses the position of the planets at the time of a subject's birth to determine personality traits. It also deals with how the planets interact with one another and influence people.

Carromancy is done by reading candle wax. There are two main methods for performing carromancy. The first is to light a candle a wait for it to melt a bit. Then, the candle is held over a bowl of cold water and the shapes that the wax solidifies in dictates the message. The other popular method is to put a piece of wax into boiling water and then reading the shapes the wax forms.

Clairvoyance is a general term for a metaphysical ability to interpret or "see" that which most cannot. There are several types of clairvoyance that deal with different senses. **Clairaudience** is a form of clairvoyance that manifests as auditory sensations. **Precognition** is a type of psychic ability that allows the practitioner to discover information about the future.

Numerology is the study of numbers and their relationships with one another as well as their correspondent traits. Numeric values within names and words can also be analyzed through numerology.

Ouija Boards are well-known divination tools. In the mid 1800's, a fad called Spiritualism overtook America. The stars of this movement were Mediums, some of whom were authentic, and some who were con artists looking to make a buck off of the trend. These fake mediums had certain tricks which led witnesses to believe that a genuine connection to the dead existed. These tricks included manipulating the table at the center of the session to move and make noises at certain points.

One of the most prevalent tools used in almost all Medium sessions of the time was the planchette. These planchettes looked like the ones used on modern Ouija boards but had two small wheels at one end and a pencil at the tip. The planchette was supposed to be moved by a spirit or entity to produce a message in writing.

The problem with the planchette was that the writing often came out indecipherable and was difficult for spirits to manipulate. This lead to the creation of the "Talking Board", or as we know it, the Ouija Board. Ouija Boards were easy to make and easy to use. People no longer needed Mediums so facilitate their spirit communications. All someone had to do to operate it was to put it on a flat table or on their lap, place the tips of their fingers on the corners of the now pencil-less planchette, and as "Are there any communications?".

Charles Kennard and William H.A. Maupin patented the Ouija Board in 1891 and turned it into a toy. It is said that the name came from asking the board itself what it was called. It responded "Ouija", which means "good luck" in ancient Egyptian, but William Fuld's account claims that the name comes from a combination of the French and German words for "yes" (Fuld took over production of the Ouija Boards in 1901). The first boards manufactured by Kennard and Maupin sold for $1.50 or $38.92 today.

One thing remained the same from the first incarnation of the Ouija Board until the present day - the use of a planchette. Without the planchette, the board is useless. It is believed that separating the two from each other can prevent any unwanted spirits from using the board as a portal and it effective is disarming the tool altogether.

The difference between Ouija boards and other divination methods such as pendulums is that Ouija boards use a spirit's energy to work, whereas pendulums use your energy. Think of it like this, Ouija boards are an open Circle, like a

"C" that needs another entity's energy to make it work. Pendulums are a closed circle like an "O", it is a closed circuit between you and the pendulum. It is not a portal or an entryway for anything to come into your divination. This is why a Ouija board's planchette only moves if there is a spirit present.

Palm reading, another well-known form of divination, is the act of determining characteristics of a person based on the physical creases on the palm of their hands. The five major lines that are studied during a palm reading are the head line, the life line, the heart line, the sun line, and the fate line.

Pendulums have been used for centuries by diviners to read energies. A pendulum is usually made of an object with some weight to it, such as a crystal or piece of metal, that comes to a point at the bottom. This object is attached to a string or chain. One uses a pendulum by holding the end of the chain or string and hovering the pendulum over a mat. Indicates "Yes" while the horizontal line indicated "No. The line in between the two is labeled "Ask Again" or "Maybe". A pendulum mat typically has three lines crossed over one another in the center. The direction that the pendulum swings in indicates the answer.

When the pendulum is held steady over the mat, the diviner may ask it a "yes-or-no" question (this does not need to be done verbally). The pendulum then swings in the direction of the answer to the question. The pendulum acts as a conduit for the energies of the universe when, in conjunction with the energy of the practitioner, is powered to retrieve the answer from the greater energy network of the universe.

Psychometry is a type of scrying that is done by sensing energy from objects, images, and other items that have come into contact with the person/thing you are trying to gather information about. The term was coined in 1842 by Dr. Joseph Rhodes Buchanan. Buchanan put forth the idea that all things in the world give off energies.

Psychometry, while not a particularly popular form of divination, has proven to be effective when done by those with experience and talent for it. Several notable Psychics have used Psychometry when working with law enforcement agencies (Such as Rosemarie Kerr). The notion that all objects retain at least a tiny bit of the energy of the person who possessed them is a foundation of Witchcraft , and in this sense, Psychometry is closely linked to energy works of many kinds.

Pyromancy deals with the movement of fire and flames. The most basic form of pyromancy can be practiced by simply observing the flickering of a flame, but other forms including casting salt into a flame to produce colors of images (**alomancy**), reading smoke produced by flames (**capnomancy**), and reading cracks in bone that has been burned (**osteomancy**).

Scrying is a form of divination that entails "seeing" a message or image within an object, such as a mirror or crystal ball. Many practitioners use meditation to put themselves into a trance-like state in which they are more able to recognize messages in their scrying object.

Tarot cards are probably the divination methods most often shown in pop culture. A deck of tarot cards contains two different types of cards, or *arcana,* the minor arcana and the major arcana. The suits in a tarot deck differ from the suits in a deck of playing cards (ie clubs, hearts, etc) and include wands, swords, cups, and pentacles/coins. The minor arcana are numbered 1-10, while the major arcana have titles associated with them such as The Magician, The High Priestess, and The Fool.

In order to read Tarot, one must become acquainted with their card deck. This can be done by cleansing the deck and then shuffling them repeatedly in order to transfer one's energy to them and become comfortable touching the cards. Once a deck is thoroughly shuffled, the diviner should cut the deck with their left hand and take the top half of the deck away. Then, they must select the number of cards they wish from the new pile created from the bottom half of the deck. The order in which these cards are drawn fit into whatever deck spread the diviner chooses to use.

Tasseography, also known as **tea leaf reading**, is the act of using herbs and boiling water to receive prophecies or messages. This is performed by sprinkling dried leaves in a cup and then pouring boiling water over them. Once the tea is sufficiently cooled, the diviner drinks the tea and then reads the leaves based on how they fall when the tea is finished.

Spirit Work

Working with spirits can be rewarding, but also extremely dangerous. Whenever one is dealing with outside forces, there are precautions that must be taken. One must first cleanse themselves as well as the space in which they will be working. Then, protection Magick should be used to ensure spirits or entities cannot harm or penetrate the practitioner.

There are several kinds of entities that spirit workers can communicate with. The most common are ghosts. **Ghosts** are the lingering energies or spirits of living things that have died. Emotions felt during life can sometimes leave behind energy impressions in this world. The presence of this energy is known as a residual haunting and can take the form of recurring movements, lingering scents or sounds, and even emotions that can be felt by others when they visit a certain place.

Sentient spirits are ghosts who interact with the living in meaningful ways. These spirits can send messages through electronic devices and will sometimes appear to the living in a physical form. Sentient ghosts can sometimes be powerful enough to manipulate objects. Ghosts are oftentimes not malicious entities and seek out those with open minds and natural tendencies toward Mediumship.

Demons are paranormal entities that are thought of as being evil or insidious. There are several different religions that believe in the existence of demons. Demons are said to infiltrate the world of the living in order to corrupt or harm humans. They themselves were never humans and this is the main difference between demons and ghosts.

Spirits can be mischievous, playful, and helpful, but also ill-intentioned. Some believe that demons can disguise themselves as ghosts, sometimes of loved ones of the practitioner, in order to lure human beings in order to do them harm. This is part of the reason why proper protections precautions must always be taken.

Though there are risks to working with supernatural entities, there are many benefits and rewards as well. Contacting ancestors or those that one knew in life who have passed on can help people heal, come to terms with death, and receive important messages from the "other side".

Some Witches choose to contact spirits that they have had no previous contact or existing relationship with. These relationships often need time to build and can be location-dependent. For example, if a spirit resides in a certain location, the practitioner will often have to go to the spirit in order to contact them.

Witches can contact spirits for companionship, conversation, or in order to discover information. These entities can sometimes offer insight into the "other side" or even information about the future.

For some, spirit communication comes naturally, but most Witches have to practice and refine their methods. Some people encounter spirits by accident, and this is mainly due to circumstance and "openness".

For example; this is how I encountered my first spirit.

When I was around 19 years old, I was riding in the passenger seat of a friend's car. It was summertime and the heat of the day had given way to rain as the sun set. It soon became completely black out as we continued on, driving to nowhere in particular through the secluded forest roads.

As we wound around the back roads, cutting through the steady rain, we came upon an old bridge. The bridge sat far above a man-made lake and waterfall called Split Rock. The road of the bridge was made of gravel with large indents spotting the entire stretch. These small craters had become puddles due to the rain and the small car had to go slowly, dipping and bucking as it moved from puddle to puddle, sending puddle water splashing away to the sides of the bridge.

The bridge was only wide enough for one car to maneuver at a time, and it became very obvious that we were the only ones on this road for a substantial distance. As we passed by the small brick guardhouse nestled on a concrete slab on the right side of the bridge, I saw a tall man in a white guard uniform standing on the left side of the building. He was standing right next to the boarded-up window closest to the road on the other side of the chain-link fence. I thought it was odd that he would still be there so late and hoped that he wasn't required to stand out in the drizzling rain.

As we left the bridge and continued down the road my companion started to tell me all these weird stories about Split Rock Road. Apparently, it was not uncommon for children to dive too deep in the lake and be tragically sucked into the artificial waterfall from the vent under the water. Some drowned trying to get unstuck from it. People have died jumping from the bridge into the lake, both on purpose and by accident.

Strangest of all is the claim that an Albino Cult (which actually did reside in northern NJ until the 1980's) used the bridge to trap cars by blocking each side of the bridge so they could butcher the passengers. There are other stories that I have found out about since this drive, including that a girl in a white dress wanders the bridge and a legend that claims if you turn off your car in the middle of the bridge, you'll die.

After he told me a few of these stories I said: "Well, then it's good that they have a guard stationed there to keep kids from doing something stupid." He was confused and told me "There's no guard there. The guard house has been abandoned for years."

Appearances of full-bodied apparitions, such as the one I saw on that night, are considered to be rare. Object manipulation, electronic interferences, and partial apparitions are seen more frequently. Many believe that supernatural entities appear to those who are more likely to accept the experience, which would make Witchcraft practitioners fairly likely to have a paranormal experience at one point or another.

Technology-Based Witchcraft

With technology being such a huge part of everyday life for most, it's no wonder than aspects of it have crept into the practice of Witchcraft . Though some practitioners look down upon this form of spellcasting, it is no less valid than any other form of Witchcraft . This is because no matter what tools are used, energy and intention are by far the most powerful and important part of Magick.

One popular form of what has been dubbed "Tech Witchcraft " is the use of emoji spells. As most know, emojis or emoticons are small pictures that are used in text messages and on social media to convey feelings, thoughts, and represent objects in the digital world. Emoji spells usually contain emojis that pertain to the intention of the spell and when shared or sent the spell is cast.

Another form of tech Magick is the art of creating sigils or Magickal symbols and illustrations with the use of computer programs and animation. Though hand-drawing sigils has been part of Witchcraft for a long time, using new-age means of creation does not hinder the effectiveness of the product.

The World of Witchcraft

Witch Classifications, Religious Aspects, & Building Your Craft

Classification of Witches

Practitioners of Witchcraft generally have certain elements of practice that they tend to gravitate toward more than others. For some, incorporating baking or cooking into their craft or working mainly with water comes naturally. For most, it takes some time and experimentation to discover what activities or elements work the best for them. When trying to figure out what type of Witch one is, it always helps to try out several different practices to discover what one connects with or has a knack for. Though many choose to identify as a certain kind of Witch, it is not mandatory or imperative that one chooses a category to fit one's practice into. The following constitute only a small sampling of various types of Witchcraft .

Eclectic Witchcraft encompasses many different aspects of Witchcraft , usually with the practitioner gathering different pieces of several classifications and melding it into a personalized and unique practice and belief system.

Elemental Witches focus on the four natural elements, Earth, Air, Fire, and Water, in their practice. These Witches collect natural objects like rocks, dirt, and stream water to bring themselves closer to the elements.

Green Witches find themselves drawn to forestry, plants, flowers, and shrubs. One distinct characteristic of a Green Witch is an emotional connection to plants and an ability to detect the energies of individuals. Green Witches may also be more likely to notice and/or interact with Magickal beings that reside in forests, such as fairies, gnomes, and pixies.

Hedge Witches are those who focus on traveling or projecting to the so-called "otherworld". Hedge Witches also engage in spirit communication and can also specialize in healing and/or mediumship. Balancing the human world and the spirit world is key in practicing Hedge Witchery and safety precautions should always be used when interacting with spirits (more on that later).

Hereditary Witches are those who are born into Magick-practicing families. Often these people will have certain inherited gifts or tendencies toward particular practices. All Hereditary Witches are born into families that have a history of Witchcraft that is passed down throughout the ancestral line, but not all Hereditary Witches choose to practice the same kind of Witchcraft as their elders. In cases like these, the Witch chooses to pursue their own craft and identifies as a different classification.

Kitchen Witches perform most of their Magick while cooking or baking. Working with herbs in the form of seasonings and brewing tea are typical activities that Kitchen Witches engage in and feel comfortable doing. For those who feel drawn to this particular type of practice, it is important to know the properties and associations of different foods like fruits and vegetables.

Music Witches focus their craft on the auditory. Spells can sometimes take the form of melodies or chants in this type of Magick. Music Witches also feel energy from music that others may not detect.

Sea Witchcraft is practiced by those who feel a strong connection to the ocean. Gathering and using material from the sea, such as salt water, sand, and seashells, is common among Sea Witches. These Witches may feel re-energized by their proximity to the ocean.

Secular or Non-Theistic Witches practice using methods and tools that are integral to Magick, such as crystals, herbs, etc. They differentiate themselves from other practices by choosing to exclude deity worship from their personal and religious beliefs. Secular Witches do not leave offerings, communicate or worship Gods or Goddesses.

Solitary Witches choose to practice exclusively on their own and without participation or interference from others. These

Witches do not join organizations or covens and feel content growing their practice without major outside influence.

Space Witchcraft is practiced by those with an intense interest or emotional/energetic connection to outer space. Space Witches keep track of the movements of the planets as well as moon phases and constellations. Space Witchcraft is also closely tied with Astrology.

Storm Witches, also known as Weather Witches, work with energy created by or contained within storms. Rain is a common tool in a Storm Witch's arsenal and can be collected for use in a wide variety of Magickal activities.

Tech Witches use modern technology to enhance or facilitate their practice. These Witches may use phone applications in conjunction with their Witchcraft and use online resources to further their knowledge and organize their Grimoire.

Urban Witchcraft centers around Magick that can be practiced within a city setting. Witches who live in urban areas often build their practice around living in a fast-paced and sometimes greenery-deficient environment.

Empaths, while not technically their own category of Witches, are people who naturally sense the emotions of others. Empaths may physically feel the emotions of others that they are around or have a bond with. It can sometimes be difficult for Empaths to differentiate their own emotions from those that they pick up from others. Empaths often need time alone to center themselves or "re-charge" after being in social situations.

Religion and Witchcraft

The relationship between religion and Witchcraft is complicated and often misunderstood. Popular belief holds that Witchcraft itself is a religion or that it is exclusively tied to often-stigmatized religious belief systems like Wicca and Satanism, but this is a misconception. Witchcraft is a spiritual practice that can be combined with almost any formal religion or belief system. In recent years, Christian Witchcraft has become popular among western Magick practitioners who were either raised in a branch of that religion or embraced it later in life.

A key aspect of blending religion and Witchcraft is to regard the natural world as a work of the higher being at the center of one's religion. Because Witchcraft centers around nature and the energies that pulse through the planet and universe, it makes sense that working with these elements also honors the creator(s) of them.

Think of it as if you were a baker making cupcakes. Witchcraft if the flour, sugar, butter, and eggs and religion is the flavor incorporated into the batter. The final product is something rich, fulfilling, and suited to the individual.

This being said, religious Witchcraft is not the best fit for everybody. Secular or non-theistic Witchcraft is just as valid as Witchcraft that includes deity worship. The inclusion of Gods and Goddesses in one's practice is a personal choice.

Altars

An altar can be an extremely personal space for a Witch. It is an area where a practitioner often keeps their tools. Some Witches like to change or rearrange their altars depending on the season or Sabbat. In addition, some Witches perform to maintain a constant configuration on their altar or design it to feature their personally preferred tools.

Witches who choose to worship deities often incorporate shrines and offerings into their altars. Every Witch's altar is unique to their practice, aesthetic tastes, and objectives. While altars are common, one does not need one to practice Witchcraft .

Sabbats

Sabbats are holidays that mark certain times of the year. Though Pagan and Wiccan practitioners are best known for celebrating the Sabbats, many Witches choose to mark them as well regardless of specific belief system. Each Sabbat has its own meaning and traditions. The northern hemisphere and the southern hemisphere celebrate the Sabbats at different times because they are season dependent. Therefore, when it is winter in the northern hemisphere, it is summer in the southern hemisphere.

Yule is the celebration of Midwinter. Plants such as Ivy, Holly, and Pine are used to decorate the home and treats including cakes, cider, fruits, pork dishes, and roasted apples are served. Yule marks the shortest and darkest day of the year and is a time to plan for the future.

Because Yule and the Christian holiday of Christmas have become linked in the past handful of millennia. Unsurprisingly they now share common traditions and associations. The colors attributed to Yule include red, green, gold, silver, and orange.

Imbolc takes place between Yule and Ostara and marks the start of the Spring season. Imbolc originated in Gaelic culture and had been celebrated since at least the 5th century. For Witchcraft practitioners, Imbolc is a holiday centered around growth, renewal, and fertility. Foods made from sunflower seeds, poppy seeds, and dairy products are common fare at an Imbolc celebration. Colors associated with Imbolc include white, pink, red, yellow, green, and brown. Flowers are used to decorate during Imbolc and a popular activity is the making of Brighid's crosses.

Ostara is the Sabbat that marks the spring equinox. Ostara centers around the rebirth of life from the darkness of the winter months. Fertility and growth are central concepts in celebrating the return of spring. Spring flowers are often incorporated into celebrations and the colors green, white, and yellow are often present. Food items such as eggs, honey cakes, and chocolate are usually consumed during this time.

Outdoor activities are popular to honor this Sabbat. Egg decoration and birdhouse building are appropriate crafts to indulge in for Ostara.

Beltane, like Imbolc and Ostara, is a spring fertility celebration. Of the three Beltane is the final. It traditionally marks the beginning of summer. Beltane's counter Sabbat is Samhain, which occurs in the fall. While Samhain celebrates the "darkness" (winter) of the year and is associated with death, Beltane celebrates the bright seasons and is associated with life.

Beltane is closely associated with fertility, sexuality, and marriage. The May Pole had a prominent part in the festivities and was traditionally danced around by the young members of the community in the early morning of Beltane. Common color correspondences include pink, white, yellow, and brown.

Litha marks midsummer and the longest day of the year. The sun is traditionally worshipped or appreciated during this time and fire is often used in rituals. Romantic relationships are often formalized during this time through weddings or other ceremonies. Parental love and the nurturing of young ones is also tied to Litha, as life in the form of crops and newborn animals is in the midst of flourishing. Blessings and spells to usher in victory are ideal during this time. The colors gold, green, and red are often used in Litha decorations.

Lammas is celebrated when summer begins to change into autumn. Lammas celebrates fruitfulness and the harvest of summer crops. Bread making and the weaving of corn stalk dolls are common activities during this time. The colors orange, brown, gray, and red are prevalent during Lammas.

Mabon, also known as the "Second Harvest", celebrates the autumnal equinox. Traditionally, Mabon is a time to give thanks for the harvest of the year. Wine-making, apple picking, and baking are appropriate activities to celebrate Mabon. Colors used in rituals and spells during this time include purple, maroon, and yellow.

Samhain (pronounced Sah-Win) is arguably the most popular of the Sabbats. Like Yule, it has become associated with holidays from several cultures, including that of Halloween. Possibly the most important aspect of Samhain is the long-held belief that the separation, or "veil", between the world of the living and that of the dead, is the thinnest on this Sabbat. Samhain marks the final harvest of the year and the beginning of winter. Traditionally, Samhain is a time to honor ancestors and connect with those who have passed on.

Offerings to the dead are usually made on Samhain and include apples, wine, and pumpkins. The concept of rebirth through death is celebrated during this Sabbat. The colors black, orange, white, and silver are used in rituals and decoration.

Familiars

Familiars are animal companions that assist in a Witch's practice. In the past, people believed that a Witch's familiar was a conduit of the Witch themselves or even a demon that acted as an assistant to a Witch. Some believe that a familiar is one spirit that takes the form of different animals over time.

There is a large difference between beloved pets and familiars, as pets often will not exhibit an interest in a Witch's practice or Magickal attributes. A familiar may watch over spells and ceremonies with intent, bring gifts such as leaves, sticks, or rocks, and show signs of spirit detection.

The connection between Witch and familiar is one that is unique and noticeably different from that of an average pet. There are often unspoken and untaught understandings and a kinship that is hard to explain to those who have not experienced it.

Covens

Social Witches may find themselves forming or seeking out a coven. Joining a coven can provide a sense of community and support that some Witches benefit from. It can also be a good environment in which to learn and grow.

Many Witches choose to become a part of a coven at one point or another. Unfortunately, many Witches come into contact with covens that foster toxic practices and relationships between members. The following are a few warning signs that a coven may be toxic.

1. New members are belittled and treated as inferior to established members.

If you join a coven and are silenced, treated as a novice (if you are not one), ordered to perform menial tasks for other members, and/or given fewer rights within the group you should carefully consider whether this coven will help you grow as a Witch or if it will hinder your education and personal practice.

2. Coven leaders demand unreasonable amounts of time dedicated to the coven.

Coven leaders can make or break the health of a coven. If a coven leader demands that a Witch be available to them at all times or deliberately violates a Witch's agreed upon participation commitment that may be a sign that the coven and its leader are too demanding of its members. There is always a time commitment associated with being a member of a coven, however, members should not be required to live their lives around the coven's needs. Covens should strive to be a supportive and mutually beneficial spiritual group, and that includes respecting members' other commitments.

3. The coven limits the type of Witchcraft that members can practice.

Some covens are specialized, and that is perfectly okay. However, if a coven tries to regulate or dictate the type of

Magick that its members practice and study on their own time it could be a red flag. The benefits of being in a coven rarely outweigh the hindrance of having one's practice limited by others.

4. Coven leaders place more importance on serving them than on practicing your craft.

The majority of problems that Witches encounter when joining a new coven usually have to do with the intentions and goals of the coven leader(s). Unfortunately, some Witches start covens or choose to lead covens to benefit their ego more than to benefit their fellow Witches. You may be able to spot a leader like this if you notice that they focus on their own practice during lessons or coven time rather than on the development of their coven members and/or insist on being treated in an exceptional manner.

5. The coven limits your social contact outside of your practice.

If the rules of a coven prevent a Witch from interacting with their family, friends, co-workers, or acquaintances in the way that they normally would then that coven should be joined with caution. Healthy social interactions outside of one's practice are important to mental and emotional well being and a coven should not interfere with the social lives of its members.

Spells

"Don't Rain on My Parade"

A weather diverting spell for when you need a sunny day.

Ingredients:

Rainwater (Or any water from a natural source)
Sand/Dirt
An item to represent the area you wish to remain rain-free

Instructions:

1. Take your sand or dirt and form it with your hands. Make a mound in the center and a moat around the mound with a pathway leading away.

2. Transfer your energy and desire for the rain to stay away to your chosen item through physical touch

3. Place your item on the center mound and slowly pour your water into the moat around the mound

4. Guide the water out of the moat while envisioning the location as you wish it will be

5. Once the water has moved around and out hold on to the item until the day in question arrives.

"Not Gonna Carry it All"

A Sachet Spell to combat gaslighting.

Ingredients:

Dried Violet
Dried Rosemary
Blue Lace Agate
Salt
A Key
A Black Bag/Sachet

Instructions:

1. Combine all ingredients into the black sachet

2. Keep the sachet under your pillow or mattress to bring you clarity and protection while you sleep. All confusion and manipulation will be absorbed into the sachet and leave you clear mentally and emotionally

3. Cleanse the Blue Lace Agate and Key every full moon. Replace the herbs and salt as needed

"Blue"

A spell to regain confidence after a breakup.

Ingredients:

Rose Quartz
A bowl of moon water
A fire-safe bowl
Dried rosemary
A small black cloth

Instructions:

1. Start by transferring any sad, mournful, angry, or hurt energies to your Rose Quartz through your favorite charging method.

2. Once you feel the Rose Quartz is charged with the emotions you wish to rid yourself of, submerge it in your bowl of moon water.

3. Next, fill your fire-safe bowl with dried rosemary and set the herb on fire until it is completely blackened or charred.

4. Scrape the rosemary ash into the black fabric and fold it closed.

5. Take the Rose Quartz out of the water and let it dry on top of the folded black cloth.

6. Once the Rose Quartz is dry, put it somewhere on your person and take the black cloth and its contents to a crossroads.

7. When at a crossroads, open the black cloth and let the ash scatter into the wind. You may clean or dispose of the black cloth after.

"Tag, You're It"

For when you need to throw harm inflicted on you back to the offender and restore balance.

Ingredients:

A Mirror
One White Candle
One Black Candle
A Sigil
Sea Salt
Dried Thyme
A Writing Utensil (preferably a marker)

Directions:

1. Draw your chosen sigil onto the center of your mirror. Add the name of the offender at the bottom of the sigil.

2. Cover the sigil in a sprinkling of dried thyme and sea salt.

3. Stand your candles on the mirror at either side of the sigil (it helps to lean taper candles toward the sigil).

4. Light your black candle, then your white candle.

5. Let the melting wax from your candles completely cover the sigil. Do not distinguish them before the sigil is covered.

6. Smother the flames to extinguish them or let the candles burn completely.

7. If you can manage it, separate the dried melted wax from the mirror. Keep it until the balance is restored.

"Tempest in a Teacup"

For when you feel yourself overreacting and want to calm down.

Ingredients:

A Sponge
A Container of Water
Lavender Essential Oil or Liquid Scent
A Calming Sigil of Your Choice
Something To Draw With, Preferably Marker
Liquid Soap

Directions:

1. Take your sponge and your writing utensil. Draw your chosen sigil on the sponge.

2. Take your container of water. Add 4 drops of your essential oil and 2 drops of your liquid soap. Place it next to your sponge.

3. Slowly submerge your sponge in your container of liquid. As it fills with water envision your anxiety flowing from your fingers and into the sponge, making it heavy and making you lighter.

4. Rub the sponge and breathe evenly and deeply as the sigil fades from the sponge.

"Ritual to Invite Spirit Contact"

This spell is designed to let a specific spirit know that you are open to communication. It includes protective elements to avoid attracting negative entities.

Ingredients:

Dried Rose Hip (2 or more)
Clove incense
Dandelion (one stem and flower)
Mint leaf or scent, in any natural form
An item that relates to the spirit you wish to contact
A Brown or White candle

Directions:

1. Light your Clove incense and your candle.

2. Sit with your item in your hand. Rub it clockwise.

3. Picture the spirit as you know it in your mind. Verbalize your openness to receiving communications (if you are unable to verbalize this or do not feel comfortable you can think it instead).

4. Take your rose hip and dandelion. Wrap them together (with string or cloth). Bury them under your doorstep (if you do not have a traditional doorstep you can put it on your porch, hang it in your doorway, or bury it by an entrance).

5. Leave a window or door open (it could be slightly open or fully open) for one hour.

6. Be sure to pay attention to little signs and happenings after performing this ritual and be sure to try and remember your dreams!

Pet Funerary Spell"

This spell is to be done soon after the death of a pet. It is to help the owner heal and to send the animal's spirit love in the afterlife.

Ingredients:

Your pet's favorite treat and/or a piece of their fur (if they have fur)
1 piece of purple fabric (size does not matter)
1 piece of brown fabric (size does not matter)
A piece of string, yarn, or thin rope.
A piece of paper
A pen or pencil

Directions:

1. Take your purple and brown fabric and lay them side by side and overlapping.

2. Put your pet's favorite treat/fur in the middle of the fabric.

3. Write your pet's name and a message for them (optional) on a piece of paper.

4. Put the piece of paper with the treat/fur.

5. Roll the items up however you'd like.

6. Tie the bundle up with your string/yarn/rope.

7. Find a peaceful spot to bury the bundle.

8. Bury the bundle and concentrate on sending your love to your pet as you fill in the hole.

9. Know that it is okay to grieve for a pet as much as you would for a human. Your grief and sadness are completely valid.

"Simple Spell to Attract a Lover"

Ingredients:

Fire
Rose Quartz
Two Candles, 1 Red and 1 Pink
Paper
A Writing Utensil
Dried Lavender

Directions:

1. Light your pink and red candles. Write the initials of your intended lover on a small scrap of paper. Take the dried lavender and the paper and burn them to ashes. Roll your rose quartz in the ash and use it to draw lines on your pulse points and over your heart.
2. Lay down and place the quartz on your forehead in between your eyebrows and invasion your next encounter with this future lover. Picture the electricity leaving your fingertips when you touch the person. Release your desire and affection into the world through your forehead and the crystal.
3. Carefully remove the rose quartz when you feel relieved of any burdening energy and slowly get up.

"Entwinement Spell"

A spell to bring two lovers closer together

Ingredients:

1 pink candle
1 red candle
4 white candles
A dish or box
Lavender (on a stem)
Fennel (on a stem)
Amber OR Jasper
Amethyst

Directions:

1. Place your candles three on each side, the first and third slightly more towards the middle than the second ones (which should be the pink and red candles). This should make a circle-like shape that's missing the top and bottom points.

2. In between the top two candles (that should be across from one another) place your Amber or Jasper. Then, in between the bottom two candles place your Amethyst. Place your dish or box in the center of the circle. Take your Fennel and Lavender and entwine them in each other carefully and delicately.

3. Hold the entwinement in both hands delicately. Feel their energies flowing into you, into each other, and your energy flowing into them. Think or speak the following:

"Love will come, Love will be, Bring my love closer to me"

4. Place the entwinement in the dish/box at the center of the circle and set it ablaze. If you cannot burn it, drown it in Moon/Sea/Holy water. Keep the ashes or wet herbs until the spell takes effect.

"Spell to Improve Your Sex Life"

Ingredients:

2 Red Candles
A Bit of Carnelian
Ambergris Oil (optional as it is hard to find)
Cinnamon (about 1 tbs in any form but I recommend powder)
Cleansing Water (Moon, Salt, Sea, or other)
A Picture of Your Sexual Partner (if you have a specific one)

Directions:

1. Place the red candles on either side of a non-flammable bowl. Place a piece of paper with your Lover's name written on it in the bowl. Light one, and then light the other with the first.

2. Put your Cinnamon of choice in the bowl at the center. Sprinkles a few drops of Ambergris Oil onto the Cinnamon if you have it.

3. Mix in one tablespoon of water. Rub the new mixture onto your pulse points and picture the intimate encounter you wish for.

4. Feel your sexual energy rushing to the pulse points. Breathe deeply and evenly until you feel the new energy settle.

"Lowlife Sachet"

A sachet to help better yourself for the sake of those you love.

Ingredients:

Dried Jasmine
A piece of paper with the names of loved ones written on it.
Dried Thyme
Cleansed Jade
A green cloth sachet

Directions:

1. On a Friday, combine all ingredients in your cloth sachet.

2. Hang the sachet in the doorway to the room you enter and exit most often.

Tips

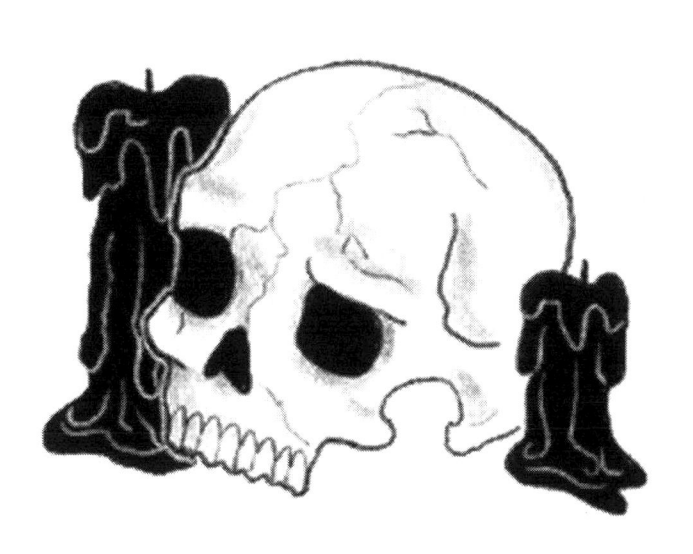

Witch Tip #101

Make sacred or holy water out of fresh snow that has fallen during the full moon

Witch Tip #102

Read! A Witch's path is one of literacy and continuously growing knowledge.

Witch Tip #103

Any object can be used for magical purposes when used with intention.

Witch Tip #104

Make your own blessing candles by warming white tea lights and sprinkling in your chosen herbs. Let the wax solidify and use them for your rituals.

Witch Tip #105

A fork can be used as a stand-in athame in a pinch.

Witch Tip #106

Salt is a great protection tool. Keep packets of it around the house for extra security.

Witch Tip #107

You are the most powerful tool that you have. Use your energy, intentions, and thoughts wisely.

Witch Tip #108
Write your wishes onto bay leaves, then burn them to help your wish reach fulfillment.

Witch Tip #109

Tie a strand of your hair to a cherry blossom tree as it blooms. This will help to attract love into your life.

Witch Tip #110

For the Witch who loves to bake: when making pies or pastries, inscribe a desired symbol into the dough to infuse your cooking with certain energies!

Witch Tip #111

If you need an energy cleansing real quick this is a simple spell to do the trick:

Light a black candle, wait until the flame is at its peak. Then take a white candle and light it with the black candle until the white candle's flame is larger than the black candle's. Then, verbalized or think of the negative energy leaving you and blow the black candle out.

You should notice a difference in the energy by the next morning!

Witch Tip #112

Not only is it important to cleanse your tools regularly, but it is equally as important to treat them with respect. Make a habit of thanking your tools when they serve you, especially pendulums and tarot cards. After all, they are your partners in Magick.

Witch Tip #113

If you're a Witch who enjoys wearing makeup, consider charging your foundations, liners, and powders. Not only can makeup be used as a sort of confidence-boosting armor, but you can also carry around positive energy right on your face!

Witch Tip #114

Don't disregard your own spells for ones you find that seem more "official". No one knows your energies and abilities better than you do, if you believe in a spell that you have created, trust yourself.

Witch Tip #115

If you're a sea Witch who doesn't often have opportunities to recharge their energy by being near the ocean, try using seaweed-infused health and beauty products, like shampoo, moisturizer, and body wash.

Witch Tip #116

If you're a Witch who grows their own herbs, or just likes to garden, and worries about their plants when they have to go away for a couple of days, try putting 2 ice cubes in the dirt around the plant before you go. The ice cubes will melt slowly and provide water to your plants while you're gone!

Witch Tip #117

Try to wait a couple of days (if you can afford to) before performing a spell, especially one that involves other people. Circumstances can change quickly and new information can surface that may change your mind.

Witch Tip #118

Before you give anyone a gift, cleanse and charge the object you are gifting with positive energy and luck for the recipient. Two gifts in one!

Witch Tip #119

Sharing pictures and documentation about your spells/rituals/etc on social media can help add power and energy to your work through the people who see them!

Witch Tip #120

If you have trouble falling asleep try to do your spell work right before bed. Doing rituals and spells will drain your energy if done properly and therefore make it easier to fall asleep.

Witch Tip #121

A potato can be used as a temporary poppet.

Witch Tip #122

Place a plum tree branch over your front door to keep out negative energy.

Witch Tip #123

Pistachios have the unique ability to help break love spells. Use unshelled pistachios in spells of this nature or (if you are not allergic) eat a pistachio during the ritual.

Witch Tip #124

Wearing a peach pit around your neck will ward off evil.

Witch Tip #125
If you don't feel comfortable using or don't want to use blood in your ritual use orange, beet, or cherry juice instead.
Witch Tip #126

Place an olive branch on your home to ward off lightning.

Witch Tip #127

Placing a slice of lemon under a visitor's chair is said to ensure a long, honest friendship.

Witch Tip #128

Put grapes on your altar when focusing on wealth and money.

Witch Tip #129

Place a fig on your doorstep before leaving for a trip to ensure that you arrive home safely.

Witch Tip #130

Place thinly sliced cucumbers on the eyelids to cure dry and swollen eyes. Put cucumber peels on the forehead to relieve headaches.

Witch Tip #131

Place an ear of corn near a sleeping infant to ward away negativity.

Witch Tip #132

To protect your home, cut a coconut in half, fill with protective herbs, seal shut again and bury somewhere on your property.

Witch Tip #133

Tie a red onion to your bedpost to protect against sickness.

Witch Tip #134

Carry a cashew with you to help increase your employment opportunities.

Witch Tip #135

Carry a Brazil nut with you to bring luck in love and settle matters of the heart.

Witch Tip #136

Carrying an avocado pit with you will cause an aura of beauty to surround you.

Witch Tip #137

Carrying an avocado pit with you will cause an aura of beauty to surround you.

Witch Tip #138

If you want to incorporate bones into your craft but have no way of obtaining them (ethically, of course) try your local pet stores! They often carry real bones and antlers that can be used in spells and altars.

Witch Tip #139

Many Witches believe that turning or stirring things clockwise (Deasil) will bring positivity, luck, and success. Using the counterclockwise (Widdershins) motion, however, can bring chaos and misfortune. These two are often reversed when practicing in the Southern Hemisphere.

Witch Tip #140

If you find yourself in a situation where you are unable to burn herbs or candles, use essential oils as a substitute.

Frequently Asked Questions

I'm not open about my craft with my family and friends. What are some easy ways to practice in secret?

This is a huge question and I'm sure I won't cover everything in this response. Here are a few tips:

- Instead of using smoke cleansing, keep a spray bottle with salt water in it and spray the corners of your room when you feel you need a protection/good energy boost.
- Bath Magick is a great way to practice on the down low. Bathing is a personal activity so it is unlikely that you will be questioned about your bath/shower time.
- Instead of having a bunch of empty and conspicuous jars in your room, keep easy-to-relocate items in them. You can keep things like pencils/pens (You can fill a new jar for each kind of writing utensil because hey, organization is important right?), Bobby pins or hair clips,

makeup/paint brushes, candles (that could also give you an excuse to be able to burn candles since they're in a jar and are not in danger of causing a fire), craft supplies, makeup like lipstick, etc.
- Take up baking or cooking. No one will question why you have so much salt/herbs around.
- Bake sigils into your food with egg wash, glaze, marinade, and dough.
- Instead of an altar, create an inspiration board or collage.
- Find a quiet and safe place outdoors to perform your rituals
- If you have or want to have Witchcraft books, they fit great in sock draws or under beds.
- If you have to do a ritual or spell that takes time and cannot be hidden, disguise it as a school project.
- Sigils are very easy to hide, draw them on your body where no one can see them.
- If you wear makeup, draw your sigils on in concealer.

- Recipe organizers are great for making a disguised spellbook
- Instead of leaving a jar of water out to be charged by the moon go for a night walk or go star-gazing and bring it along.
- Gum and mint cases are great for carrying around herbs and crystals.

How do I know if my spell worked?

Spellcasting is mostly trial and error. Start with spells that have obvious desired results, like a spell to cure a headache. If it doesn't work at first, try it again and maybe tweak it a bit. You should be able to observe the results.

Why are some Witches against cursing?

Some Witches choose not to perform curses or to share them/recommend them because of the Threefold rule (which is a bit like the Hindu/Buddhist idea of Karma). The idea is that if you perform a curse against someone, that negative energy will come back to you three times stronger. This has been experienced by many Witches, most of whom will warn against cursing. A lot of Witches do not curse because they do not want to put out or receive negativity because it could put them in danger.

How do I become a Witch?

Everyone's path in Witchcraft is different. Some grow up with elements of Witchcraft in their life, others find their way to Witchcraft . For anyone who wishes to start practicing, I recommend reading books, Witchcraft site, and blogs. Knowledge is very important in all aspects of life, but especially in Witchcraft . As a self-taught Witch, I know how much there is to be learned from doing a bit of research. So search, learn, and think. That is how you can become a Witch.

What are some simple things I can do to get started?

It depends on what you want to do. Some simple divination methods for beginners are pendulum readings and Tarot readings. With a bit of research and maybe a cheat sheet for tarot, you can get a great feel for your energies through these tools. You could also try charging certain objects like jewelry or coins or performing some basic spells.

Can I be a Witch even if none of my relatives are/were?

Absolutely! Some are born into Witchy families and can tap into their power more easily, but that does not mean that they are the only ones with Magick in them. All humans have powers of divination and Magick but few choose to access them or grow them. By starting your path into Witchcraft you are choosing to unlock your metaphysical power.

Can practicing Witchcraft or divination open you up to evil entities?

It depends on what kind of Witchcraft or divination you practice. Like Karma or the Threefold rule, everything you put into the world comes back to you. So if you choose to put negative energy out you should expect that amount of negativity or more to come back into your life. Divination methods like Tarot and Pendulums do not open you up to negative entities. This is because when using these methods you are using your own energy and not something else's. When using a Ouija board, however, you are using a spirit or other entity's energy to communicate and therefore are at risk of being attacked, invaded, or tethered to that entity. (Side note: it is a common misconception that Ouija boards themselves are dangerous. The piece that is actually responsible for communication is the triangular part called the planchette. If you own a Ouija board it is imperative that you keep the Planchette and the board separate at all times!)

Are there any alternatives to burning candles and incense? I live in a place where I am unable to light a fire or create smoke.

There are always alternatives for most things in Witchcraft . Oil warmers can be an alternative to incense, although it can produce scarce vapors. There are also websites where you can burn virtual candles and electronic candles are always a great alternative. You can also spray certain scents instead of burning candles of the same kind. These are just a couple of alternatives but there are many more.

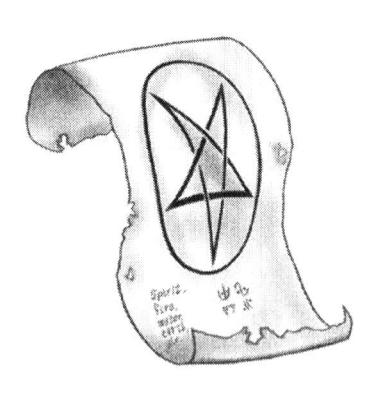

Glossary of Terms

Astral Travel/Projection: The act of separating the physical and spiritual body from one another in order to visit the Astral plane.

Astrology: The observation of planetary movements and their effects on human beings.

Anthame: A blade used symbolically in rituals such as circle casting.

Aura: A field of energy that surrounds a living thing or object. This energy can sometimes be interpreted as a color and may be used to "read" a person to determine aspects of their health, mood, or personality.

Book of Shadows: A Book of Shadows acts as a Witch's journal in which spells, tips, recipes, and charts are documented.

Charm: A Charm is an object that has been imbued with Magick and energy to serve a purpose.

Consecration: An object or place can be consecrated by cleansing and dedicating it to an objective or to the divine.

Coven: A Coven is a group of Witches that practice Magick together and often follow agreed-upon guidelines.

Equinox: A day when the sun crosses the celestial equator and the day and the night are equal.

Essential Oil: Oils extracted from plants that are concentrated. These oils usually need to be diluted before use.

Grimoire: A manual or instruction book meant to teach the practice of Witchcraft .

Hellenic Witchcraft : A form of Witchcraft that is based on ancient Greek beliefs and deities.

Incense: A mixture of resin, herbs, and essential oils that is burned to release a fragrance.

Knot Magick: A type of spellcasting based on the tying and untying of knots.

Meditation: The act of relaxing the mental state in order to relax or focus on a particular goal.

Medium: A Medium is a person who receives messages from or acts as a line of communication for spirits.

Moon Sign: A person's moon sign is dictated by the constellation that the moon passed through at the time of their birth.

Mortar and Pestle: A mortar and pestle is a pair of tools used to crush herbs, minerals, and other items in order to turn them into a powder. The mortar is a stone or ceramic bowl and a pestle is a heavy grinding or smashing tool.

Necromancy: The act of contacting the dead.

Occult: A term referring to secret or forbidden knowledge often having to do with the paranormal.

Omen: A sign of events to come. Omens can be good or bad and their meanings often depend on circumstance and cultural significance.

Poppet: Representations of individuals or ideas that are often crafted in the form of dolls.

Runes: Letter symbols from the Norse culture that are used as divination tools.

Solstice: A day when the sun is either at its highest or lowest in relation to the horizon. The summer solstice marks the longest day of the year while the winter solstice marks the shortest.

Sun Sign: A sign of the zodiac that is assigned to a person based on the position of the sun at the time of their birth.

Tincture: A combination of alcohol and herbal extracts.
Wand: A tool used in ritual Magick for focusing and pointing energy.

Ward: A protection that is created or put upon an object to deter negativity or harmful entities.

Postface

Though there is much, much more to contemporary Witchcraft than could fit in this basic guide, I want to leave you with a bit of advice. Throughout your journey as a Witch, you may at times feel discouraged, confused, and/or inadequate. During these times, please remember that every Witch, no matter how well-known or powerful, has felt the same way at some point.

One of the amazing things about Witchcraft is that even though every Witch's craft is different, there is a sense of community and of connection not just with the universe at large but with other practitioners as well. This connection comes not from physical interaction, but the mutual understanding that everything in the world is inherently intertwined in one way or another.

As Witches, we should strive to nurture these connections by being aware of our effects on others as well as on the natural world and the supernatural world. You will find that kindness begets kindness, even if it is not immediate.